Praise for *The Multiplie*

"Finally a real book for leaders to read, digest, and actually use. I cannot wait to use the specific exercises to promote the Multiplier Effect!"

**Molly Broderson, Elementary School Principal,
Hayes, Virginia**

"This provocative book is a must for school leaders. It provides clarity and insight into leadership and provides a framework to deliver strategy, improve working relationships, and boost individual leader's capacity and capability. It is packed with real-world techniques for engaging people at all levels. This is a timely contribution to the leadership debate when schools everywhere are facing the challenge of change."

Dame Pat Collarbone, Director, Creating Tomorrow

"The Multiplier concept is a powerful tool to develop and improve leaders both in business and across education, where we hear more about failure than we do about success. If educational leaders at every level read this book, we would hear more stories of successful educational outcomes. This book belongs on the reading list of anyone wanting to become the kind of leader that makes people and organizations better."

**Dean Gary Cornia, Marriott School of Management,
Brigham Young University**

"Educators are constantly looking for ways to do more with less. This book provides actionable steps that allow leaders to multiply the talents of their teachers while also fostering an exhilarating experience for staff and students alike."

**Kendra Hanzlik, Elementary School Teacher-Strategist,
Cedar Rapids, Indiana**

"Dripping in rich storytelling and anecdotes, this book explores why our society, schools, and companies desperately need to embrace the power of Multipliers in order to unleash talent, allow others agency, and fully utilize dormant intelligence. If you are looking to learn new leadership techniques, take advantage of your potential, and understand how to add value to your life and work, *The Multiplier Effect* is for you."

Nikhil Goyal, Author of *One Size Does Not Fit All* and
Forbes 30 under 30

"Do not lead or attempt to lead without reading this! It will open your eyes and change you."

Matthew Henry, CIO, LeTourneau University

"An educator's role, by definition, is multiplying genius and developing future leaders. This book is an instructional manual for educational leaders who want to ignite the genius in their schools. The authors offer a thought-provoking yet simple framework full of stories and clear principles that can be put to use immediately in an educational setting."

Prasad Kaipa, Executive Director Emeritus,
Center for Leadership, Innovation and Change,
Indian School of Business, and co-author of *Smart to Wise*

"In our hierarchical world of academic medicine, moving to the Multiplier model of leadership could be the game changer."

Darrell Kirch, M.D., President and CEO,
Association of American Medical Colleges

"*The Multiplier Effect* provides the secret sauce for what makes great teachers and leaders in education. Chock full of engaging stories, extensive research, and insightful 'experiments,' this is a must-read for anybody who cares about the future of society. Creating a Multiplier Effect in the education industry would be transformative."

Michael Moe, Founder and CEO of GSV Asset Management,
Author of *Finding the Next Starbucks* and *American Revolution 2.0:*
How Education Innovation is Going to Revitalize America and
Transform the U.S. Economy

"The mindsets and practices of the Multiplier and the Accidental Diminisher translate readily to our education system. Educators are in the Multiplier business—whether you are a superintendent, principal, board member, teacher, parent, or student, you will find this book to be a compelling read and a toolkit for school and districtwide implementation. I hope this book starts many Multiplier experiments."

Julie Wilson, Founder, Institute for the Future of Learning

THE multiplier EFFECT

TAPPING THE GENIUS INSIDE OUR SCHOOLS

LIZ WISEMAN | LOIS ALLEN | ELISE FOSTER

Foreword by **CLAYTON CHRISTENSEN**

CORWIN
A SAGE Company

FOR INFORMATION:

Corwin

A SAGE Company

2455 Teller Road

Thousand Oaks, California 91320

(800) 233-9936

www.corwin.com

SAGE Publications Ltd.

1 Oliver's Yard

55 City Road

London EC1Y 1SP

United Kingdom

SAGE Publications India Pvt. Ltd.

B 1/I 1 Mohan Cooperative Industrial Area

Mathura Road, New Delhi 110 044

India

SAGE Publications Asia-Pacific Pte. Ltd.

3 Church Street

#10-04 Samsung Hub

Singapore 049483

Acquisitions Editor: Arnis Burvikovs

Associate Editor: Desirée A Bartlett

Editorial Assistant: Mayan White

Production Editor: Laura Barrett

Copy Editor: Sarah J. Duffy

Typesetter: C&M Digitals (P) Ltd.

Proofreader: Stefanie Storholt

Indexer: Teddy Diggs

Cover Designer: Michael Dubowe

Permissions Editor: Jennifer Barron

Copyright © 2013 by Elizabeth Wiseman

All rights reserved. When forms and sample documents are included, their use is authorized only by educators, local school sites, and/or noncommercial or nonprofit entities that have purchased the book. Except for that usage, no part of this book may be reproduced or utilized in any form or by any means, electronic or mechanical, including photocopying, recording, or by any information storage and retrieval system, without permission in writing from the publisher.

All trade names and trademarks recited, referenced, or reflected herein are the property of their respective owners who retain all rights thereto.

Printed in the United States of America

A catalog record of this book is available from the Library of Congress.

ISBN 978-1-4522-7189-7

This book is printed on acid-free paper.

SFI label applies to text stock

14 15 16 17 10 9 8 7 6 5 4

Contents

Foreword

Shortly after *The Innovator's Dilemma* was published in 1997, I spent some time with Andy Grove, the CEO of Intel. At the time, Cyrix and AMD were disrupting Intel with their low-cost microprocessors. As Grove quickly grasped the theories of disruptive innovation, he saw the threat materializing and understood what Intel would have to do to survive.

I was interested though that Grove didn't come out to the company and announce from on high a strategy for Intel. Instead he established an educational seminar during which Intel's top 2,000 managers—not a small undertaking—studied the disruption model. As a result, Intel launched its Celeron chip at the bottom of its market—a disruptive strategy that was counter-intuitive to the common logic of how to make money at Intel. It was also very successful in fending off the would-be disruptors. Reflecting back on that history, Grove later told me, "The disruption model didn't give us any answers. But it gave us a common language and a common way to frame the problem so that we could reach consensus around a counterintuitive course of action."

People often wonder that if disruption is going to occur, then does leadership matter? Indeed, the answer is that when disruption is afoot, nothing could be more important for an organization than its leadership.

Currently disruption is coming to education in the form of online learning—and with it an historic opportunity to remake our schools from their factory-model roots into student-centric organizations that allow each child to realize her fullest human potential. As this disruption takes root and grows, leadership in shaping it in our schools will matter enormously.

In *The Multiplier Effect*, authors Liz Wiseman, Lois Allen and Elise Foster make a compelling case for a new, provocative approach to leadership in education. They ask the question, "Do the smartest leaders create the smartest organizations or do the seemingly smartest leaders have a diminishing effect on the intelligence of others?" They offer a model of leadership that recognizes that the critical leadership skill is not personal knowledge but the ability to tap into the knowledge of others. They reject the notion that a heroic leader, a lone innovator, or a single brain at the head of a school can solve our most complex problems. They explain why it takes more than just a genius to lead a school.

Successful leaders like Grove seem in many situations to understand how to harness the power of the people around them innately. In Grove's case, through allowing his managers to learn and grow, together they were able to steer Intel forward and innovate successfully.

That's the promise of Multipliers. They can help make an entire organization smarter and more effective. Amplifying the intelligence of the educators in a school—to embolden them by placing them in teams with the autonomy to solve problems with new processes—is critical as our schools are tasked with solving challenges for which they were not built.

Too often leaders grow frustrated with the ideas for innovation that reach their desk. They shout back at people in their organization for more innovative ideas, but what they don't see is that the problem is not with the people generating the ideas, but with the processes and priorities that exist within every single organization that morph and shape every idea to fit the capabilities of the organization instead of the original problem they were intended to solve. As a result of these processes and priorities, what comes out of the innovation funnel is me-too idea after me-too idea.

What this means is that if school leaders are to preside over schools and districts that continually innovate, then they need to shape actively these processes and priorities so they can leverage and unleash—not stifle—the strengths of their fellow educators.

The Multiplier Effect reminds us that we need to do more than innovate our classrooms. Based on three years of research and a study of over 400 educational leaders, it shows us how we need to rethink the model of leadership that will sustain innovation and deliver a more powerful and productive learning system. We need managers who go beyond just planning and executing; we need leaders who have a plan for their staff to learn and discover.

Ultimately we are all educators and learners. It shouldn't be so surprising that those schools and districts that remember and prize that might also have dramatic student successes to show for it. You *can* reinvent your school and create a multiplying culture. Remembering why we entered the profession of education in the first place and mul-tiplying the leadership around us is a great place to start.

Clayton M. Christensen

Introduction

I've always been a genius watcher, fascinated by the intelligence of others. When I began my career at Oracle Corporation, I landed in a rich stew of brilliant and interesting people. I was happy to rub shoulders with my new colleagues, hoping something would wear off on me; after all, I was voted class clown of my high school.

During my 17-year career at Oracle (where I got thrown into management at 24 years old and found myself running the corporate university), I worked closely with the senior executives, all of whom were brilliant. I saw how some leaders literally shut down brainpower in people around them, yet other leaders seemed to amplify the intelligence around them. I wondered why these smart leaders couldn't look beyond their own capacity to see and use the full capability on their teams. I could see there was more intelligence inside the organization than we were using. I suspected that there were smart, underutilized people across organizations everywhere.

I also had the honor of working with brilliant guest faculty, like CK Prahalad, the renowned strategy professor from the University of Michigan. While CK taught and consulted with Oracle, I became his student, soaking up everything I could learn from him. Years after I had been CK's client and student, I was visiting the Prahalad home. Gayatri, CK's wife, pulled me aside and whispered, "CK would never tell you this himself, so I will. CK told me that you might be the best student he has had. He thinks you are really smart." Inside I was laughing and wondering how this was possible, thinking, "Surely CK has had a thousand students who are a lot smarter than me." But then it hit me. I was smart *around* CK. When I worked with him, I felt brilliant. He made me think deeply. He made me question things and challenge assumptions. His intelligence provoked mine.

I left the Prahalad home that day thinking about what Gayatri had shared with me. I wondered why I was so smart around CK. Gayatri's gift helped me better see what I had observed for years at Oracle—that some people make us smarter. I began to wonder, "Why are we smart and capable around some people but not around others?" It is the question that spawned 2 years of research and the book *Multipliers: How the Best Leaders Make Everyone Smarter*.

The book struck a chord with managers across the business world, from the technology firms of Silicon Valley to financial institutions in the United Arab Emirates, and diverse industries in between, such as healthcare, consumer goods, the military, and education. As I have been teaching these ideas to leaders around the world, I've seen managers embrace the idea that they can get more capability from their people while also offering their employees an exhilarating work experience. As I've crisscrossed these diverse settings, I've noticed that the principles have their deepest resonance with organizations that face a confluence of conditions:

1. They are experiencing the challenges and opportunities resulting from growing demands.

2. They face resource shortages.

3. They understand that innovation is a critical strategy to meet growing demands.

4. They recognize, or merely suspect, that the old models of leadership are no longer sufficient.

Meanwhile, the *Multipliers* book website was receiving numerous comments and inquiries from schools across the United States (and beyond). It was clear that the book's ideas resonated with as many educational leaders as business leaders. We wondered if perhaps the greatest use of these ideas would be in our education system. Surely even a casual observer of global affairs can see that freedom and prosperity hinge on economic abundance and that a vibrant economy is dependent on a strong, efficacious educational system. As a mother of four children in public schools, I know that the stakes are high both for us collectively as well as for each child. So when Arnis Burvikovs from Corwin asked if I would write a version of *Multipliers* for educational leaders, I put my business research priorities aside and assembled a team to send Multipliers "straight to the principal's office."

I turned first to the educator and educational leader I admired most, Lois Allen. Lois is a former special education classroom teacher, who spent 16 years teaching the most challenging children to read and use that skill to gain knowledge. She was fascinated by the question: *How do children learn?* After encountering Roberta, a seemingly magical principal, Lois's question changed: *How do great administrators lead?* Spurred by Roberta's belief that Lois had "principal written all over her," Lois became an assistant principal, an elementary and middle school principal, and a manager of special education. Lois is also my mother. I have grown up seeing her total devotion to educating children and her devotion to leadership. In the development of this book, Lois's role was to ground our work in the realities of educators and to lead the research.

We next tapped Elise Foster, a leadership coach who teaches Multiplier leadership and who brings an analytic approach to teaching and coaching (owing in part to her background as an engineer). Elise studied leadership at the Harvard Graduate School of Education, receiving her master's in education there, and she brings a hopeful, innovative view of the future of education. As a mother of a school-age child, she's passionate about education and wants to see our education system capitalize on children's natural intellectual curiosity and not simply reduce their inquiries to multiple-choice questions. Elise, who is smart, diligent, and witty, leads our efforts to help leaders learn to become Multipliers.

The three of us are united in the goal of building Multiplier leadership across our education system. We hope to see Multipliers in staff rooms, in classrooms, in the principal's office, and most certainly in the superintendent's office. We can't provide answers to education's most vexing problems, but we offer a model of leadership to address them. We offer you the data and stories that emerged from our research. We offer you questions to help you ponder the type of leadership needed to build strong schools and smart students. We suspect, as much of the current research suggests, that great teachers make the difference. But perhaps it takes more than leaders who hire great teachers; it also takes leaders who inspire and engage teachers' abilities to their fullest.

Unlocking individual potential is not just a matter of personal will. And it is not just a matter of individual leaders, even if those leaders are Multipliers. It is a function of entire systems. This is why we need educational institutions that are Multiplier environments.

Join Lois, Elise, and me on a journey as we investigate a fundamental question: *What becomes possible when our schools and universities are led by Multipliers?* Join the exploration and discover how to unleash brilliance all around you . . . with your administrative team, with your staff, with your students, across your entire school. Then, watch the Multiplier effect grow across your entire district.

Liz Wiseman
Menlo Park, California
March 2013

To J. Bonner Richie, Dr. Margaret Naeser, Robert Kegan, and all the other educators who have taught, inspired, led, and shaped our lives.

About the Authors

 **Liz Wiseman** teaches leadership to executives around the world. She is the president of The Wiseman Group, a leadership research and development center headquartered in Silicon Valley, California. She is the author of the bestselling book *Multipliers: How the Best Leaders Make Everyone Smarter*. She has conducted significant research in the field of leadership, collective intelligence, and talent management and writes for the *Harvard Business Review* and a variety of other leadership journals. She is the former vice president of Oracle University. Liz holds a master's in organizational behavior and a bachelor's in business management from Brigham Young University. She is a frequent guest lecturer at BYU, Harvard, the Naval Academy, the Naval Postgraduate School, Stanford, and Yale. She is the mother of four school-age children.

 **Lois Allen** has 30 years of experience in public education. She is a former teacher, special education manager, assistant principal, principal (elementary and middle school), and lecturer at San Jose State University. She holds bachelor's with great distinction in speech pathology and audiology and a master's in special education, both from San Jose State University. She holds California credentials as a speech and language pathologist, a special education classroom teacher, and a school administrator as well as a Certificate of Clinical Competency from the American Speech and Hearing Association. In addition to her role as the mother of four children and grandmother of thirteen, she is an avid gardener and a community and church volunteer.

 **Elise Foster** is a leadership coach who enables education and business executives to unlock their potential to become even more successful. She has conducted significant research in the field of leadership within education systems. As the Education Practice Lead for the Wiseman Group in Silicon Valley, Elise guides senior leaders on using their intelligence to make everyone around them smarter and more capable. She has taught and coached students at Indiana University (Kelley School of Business) and as a management fellow at Harvard University. She holds a bachelor's and master's degrees in engineering from Virginia Tech and a master's in education from Harvard University. She is the mother of one school-aged daughter, and she also enjoys finding the genius in local high school students through her work with the Lilly Foundation Scholarship and Youth Leadership Bartholomew County.

1

The Multiplier Effect

*If your actions inspire others to dream more, learn more, do more,
and become more, you are a leader.*

John Quincy Adams

It is the summer of 1989 and Stephanie, wearing her brand-new interview suit from Nordstrom and clutching her newly minted master's degree from Stanford University's School of Education, soars through the doors of her new employer, the internal training department of a private college. She is full of passion and brimming with ideas, ready to put her skills and education to use in her first big job. However, by early spring her excitement dims. She has found, as many of us did early on in our careers, that her entry-level job as a training coordinator involved a daily grind of routine tasks like scheduling classrooms, ordering training supplies, and copying class evaluations and distributing them to the deans and directors.

But Stephanie's source of discouragement extended far beyond her mundane, narrow role; she was also the prey of a smart but micromanaging boss, Diane,[1] who had a knack for creating stress all around her. To Diane, it wasn't good enough to make the copies and get them distributed on time. They had to be stapled just so . . . at a 45-degree angle for one recipient and paper clipped for another. She instilled the fear of God in Stephanie, as if getting the staple wrong would bring down the entire operation. Stephanie's response was natural—she pulled back, played it safe, did the minimum. Perpetuating the vicious cycle she started, Diane began to manage more tightly, criticizing Stephanie's mistakes and comparing her to her peers. Soon Stephanie wasn't doing much of anything well. Her enthusiasm was all but extinguished.

Sensing the crisis, Diane beckoned Stephanie into her office for "a chat." She chastised Stephanie's lack of enthusiasm and lack of effort. Stephanie tried desperately to explain that her current job responsibilities were so simplistic that they only required a fraction of her abilities. She begged for something more challenging to do. Undeterred by her pleas, Diane urged her to put forth greater effort and sent the seriously discouraged Stephanie back to her desk.

This situation festered until a couple months later when the department experienced a change in leadership. A new manager, Lori,[2] was appointed from within the group, and she could see that Stephanie was extraordinarily smart, actually driven, and severely underutilized. Lori called Stephanie into her office and said, "Steph, we are spending too much time making paper copies of class evaluations. We need an online evaluation system. And I need you to build it." With that, this brand-new manager dumped a stack of software manuals into Stephanie's arms and instructed, "Learn how to use this software. Let's see if you can develop a working prototype in the next 3 months." Lori outlined detailed expectations for the project and reminded Stephanie that she still needed to do her day job in full.

With her new leader's vote of confidence in her capabilities, Stephanie's performance shifted out of a slow grind and was pushed into high gear. Something had changed and she was now on fire. Despite having no experience with computer software, other than writing papers in WordPerfect while in graduate school, she learned the inner workings of the software quickly and built the prototype. She tackled her administrative work with renewed thinking and energy. With her mind whirling with the new programming language she was learning, she even managed to remember which evaluations needed staples and which required paper clips.

The prototype that Stephanie built in 3 months further developed into a complete production system housed and supported by the information technology department. As for Stephanie, she went on to become a top-rated technology instructor.

Stephanie described this experience as "challenging but totally exhilarating." She reflected, "My passion had returned, and I could not wait for the next big challenge that Lori would throw at me. She recognized my untapped potential and drew it out, beyond anything I could have imagined on my own."

Stephanie's experience illustrates that often a change in leadership can cause a change in capability. She was smart and capable under one leader but operating at a fraction of her true capability under the other. What did her first manager say and do that so diminished her intelligence and capability? And what did the second do that restored and expanded Stephanie's abilities to think, to learn, and to perform at her best?

Sometimes with a change in leadership comes a change in capability.

Some leaders make us better and smarter. They amplify our intelligence. This book is about these leaders, who access and revitalize the intelligence in the people around them. We call them Multipliers. This book will show you why they create genius around them and make everyone, staff and students alike, smarter and more capable.

THE MULTIPLIER EFFECT

The Problem With Genius

Smart leaders don't always bring out smarts in others. Many leaders, having spent years being rewarded for their intelligence, never look beyond their own capabilities to see and use the full genius of their team. These myopic leaders can end up draining intelligence from the people around them. These leaders become Diminishers.

You know these people, because you've worked for them. They are smart leaders, but they shut down the smarts of others. They are idea killers and energy sappers. They are the ones who desperately need to prove they are the smartest person in the room. But for them to be big, others have to be small. These leaders consume so much space that they leave little room for others to contribute. They create stress and pressure that can shut down good ideas. People quickly figure out that it is just easier and safer to retreat and let the boss do all the thinking.

On the other side of the continuum are leaders who use their intelligence to amplify the smarts and capabilities of the people around them. When these leaders walk into a room, light bulbs go on over people's heads; ideas flow and problems get solved. People get smarter in their presence because they're given permission to think. These are the leaders who inspire employees to stretch themselves to deliver results that surpass expectations. These leaders seem to make everyone around them better and more capable. These leaders are like Multipliers—intelligence Multipliers.

Our educational systems need more of them, especially now when leaders are expected to do more with less.

The Research

We've all had experience with these two dramatically different kinds of leaders, and we know their effects firsthand. Many of us can recount frustrating, if not painful, experiences working under Diminishers. Hopefully you have had the chance to have the wounds inflicted by a Diminisher healed by the exhilarating salve of working with a Multiplier.

Having seen the diminishing and magnifying effect of these leaders in our schools and universities, both through our own experience and through the accounts of others, we set out to understand a fundamental question: *Why do some leaders drain intelligence while others amplify it?* We wanted to know what these Multipliers did, how they thought, and the impact they had on the intelligence and capability of people around them.

We built on Liz's original research on Multipliers in business and nonprofit organizations, in which she and Greg McKeown studied 150 leaders in 35 companies across four continents. We then took a deep dive into the education world, studying an additional 438 leaders: 330 through surveys and 108 through detailed interviews. (A full description of our research process can be found in Appendix A). We asked educational professionals, both teachers and administrators, to analyze their experiences working for Diminishers and Multipliers. Their amazing stories flowed freely.

The 2X Multiplier Effect

Not surprisingly, people told us that Multipliers got more from them than Diminishers did. We asked each person to identify the percentage of their capability being utilized with each leader. They told us that a Diminisher typically utilized between 20% to 50% of their capacity, with an average of 40%. The range for Multipliers was typically between 70% and 100%, with an average of 88%. When we compared the two sets of data, we found an even higher Multiplier Effect factor than we had expected. Multipliers got 2.3 times more! And when we factored in the responses of people who said their Multiplier got more than 100% of their intelligence (submitting responses such as 110% claiming that their intelligence actually grew), we found Multipliers got 2.4 times more.

Because Multipliers are leaders who look beyond their own genius and focus on extracting and extending the genius of others, they get more from their people. They don't get a little more; as you can see, they get vastly more. Multipliers get so much brainpower from their people that they essentially double the size of their staff for free. We call this the Multiplier Effect.

Meanwhile, Diminishers are costly. Sure, these Diminishers can get the job done, but they come at a very high cost. Why? Because they waste talent and intellect. At a time when educational organizations are expected to do more with less, leaders can't afford to overlook the intelligence and capability that sits right in front of them.

Despite their cost and their often toxic effect on school culture, why do many of these diminishing leaders remain in positions of importance? Is it because they often do a good job managing up to the superintendent and school board? Or is it because staff and teachers working for Diminishers operate in fear, retreat to a safe place, and learn to tread lightly hoping that "this too shall pass?" Or is it because they create a flurry of determined activity around them and, in absence of clear answers for our most difficult challenges in education, even the pretense of progress can be comforting? Whatever the reasons, it is time to do the math and realize that our school systems simply can't afford the cost these leaders incur.

Multipliers in Education

The need for leaders who can multiply intelligence and capability is more vital than ever. The natural response from educational leaders who are weighed down by enormous challenges and work demands include the following:

- We are already overworked.
- Our most effective staff are even more overworked.
- The only way we can make these changes is through the addition of more resources.

Yet budgets remain static, and often dwindle. Instead of pinning one's hopes on a cavalry of additional resources, a school leader might instead ask the question Paul Ainsworth, vice principal of a Leicestershire secondary school, did after reading *Multipliers*: "Are we getting the most out of our staff?" It is a very different question than "Can our staff work harder or more?"[3] With Multiplier logic, we might just find that our schools' new challenges can be met, not by rehiring more resources, but by better utilizing the brainpower that currently exists in our organizations.

No one would dispute the statement that there are many challenges, both old and new, facing our educational systems today. Declining financial support to our schools paired with increased demands for academic performance and accountability are straining the very fiber of our educational organizations, not to mention the stress that is heaped daily on our teachers and administrators. Despite public and private resources that are being poured into safety net programs, we still have students exiting elementary school lacking the reading skills to be academically successful. As graduation standards are being raised, dropout rates are increasing. Twenty-two percent of all American children live in poverty according to 2010 Census Bureau data[4]; too many students arrive at school hungry. How do we prepare students for the information age? How do we keep good teachers? Is school choice the answer? Are charter schools the answer? Is privatization of our public schools the answer? There are a myriad of questions but no simple answers.

We can't even agree on what needs help. We debate such questions as: Is it our educational systems that need fixing, or is it our societal systems that need a fix? One thing is for sure: Our educators are carrying a weighty load and could use some help. Our educators need more than blame.

The intent of this book is not to offer fixes to the problems. Our purpose is to offer educational leaders a model of leadership that will enable them to address these challenges by more fully engaging the intelligence resources that lie within their schools, districts, or provinces. What could you accomplish if you got twice as much from your administrative staff or from your teachers? What if every assistant principal was allowed to lead as if he or she was the principal? What if teachers felt free to hold nothing back and be their absolute best both in their classrooms and in taking leadership roles in their schools? What becomes possible if the entire staff is functioning at 100% of their intellectual capacity?

To find answers, we must see that multipliers think differently. They approach leadership differently. They get dramatically enhanced results. Here's how they utilize others at their fullest.

THE FIVE DISCIPLINES OF THE MULTIPLIER

In analyzing data on more than 400 educators, we uncovered several areas where Multipliers and Diminishers operate quite similarly. They both are outcome focused. And both have strong instructional judgment and educational insights. However, as we searched the data for the active ingredients unique to Multipliers, we found five disciplines in which Multipliers differentiate themselves from Diminishers.

1. Attract and Optimize Talent

Multipliers lead people by operating as Talent Finders, whereby they tap into people's natural talents regardless of their seat in the building. People stay loyal to them not because they feel obligated, but rather because they know they will grow and be successful. In contrast, Diminishers operate as Gatekeepers, by putting people into boxes, insisting that staying within the boundaries results in greater productivity. They tend to protect people and control resources, creating artificial restrictions that hamper effective use of all resources, and they overlook what is possible. People may initially be attracted to work with a Diminisher, but it is often the place where people's careers die. The Diminisher is a Gatekeeper. The Multiplier is a **Talent Finder**.

2. Create Intensity That Requires Best Thinking

Multipliers establish a unique and highly motivating work environment where everyone has permission to think and the space to do their best work. Multipliers operate as Liberators, producing a climate that is both comfortable and intense. They remove fear and create the safety that invites people to do their best thinking. But they also create an intense environment that demands people's best effort. In contrast, Diminishers operate as Tyrants, introducing a fear of judgment that has a chilling effect on people's thinking and work. They demand people's best thinking, yet they don't get it. The Diminisher is a Tyrant. The Multiplier is a **Liberator**.

3. Extend Challenges

Multipliers operate as Challengers by seeding opportunities, laying down a challenge that stretches an organization, and generating belief that it can be done. In this way, they drive themselves and the organization to go beyond what was previously thought possible. In contrast, Diminishers operate as Know-It-Alls, pushing their personal initiatives and method to flaunt their genius, thus never asking their organization to do things they can't do themselves. While Diminishers set direction, Multipliers ensure direction gets set. The Diminisher is a Know-It-All. The Multiplier is a **Challenger**.

4. Build Community Decisions

Multipliers make decisions in a way that informs and readies the organization to execute those decisions. They function as Community Builders, operating with transparency and constructing debate and decision-making forums to drive sound decisions. As a result they build an organization that understands the issues and can quickly support and execute the decision. In contrast, Diminishers operate as Decision Makers who make decisions efficiently within a small inner circle, but they leave the broader organization confused, which just delays the discussion. In reality, every decision in your school gets debated either upfront or post decision. The Diminisher is a Decision Maker. The Multiplier is a **Community Builder**.

5. Instill Ownership and Accountability

Multipliers are Investors who demand excellence and give ownership while providing resources necessary for success. This results in strong, trusting relationships. In contrast, Diminishers are Micromanagers who get the job done alone and are often successful in spite of themselves. The problem is that things don't get done without them and they become a bottleneck. The school staff spends its time seeking approval, rather than educating. The Diminisher is a Micromanager. The Multiplier is an **Investor**.

THE 5 DISCIPLINES OF THE MULTIPLIERS

Diminishers			Multipliers	
The Gatekeeper	Hoards resources and underutilizes talent		The Talent Finder	Attracts talented people and uses them at their highest point of contribution
The Tyrant	Creates a tense environment that suppresses people's thinking and capability		The Liberator	Creates an intense environment that requires people's best thinking and work
The Know-It-All	Gives directives that showcase how much they know		The Challenger	Defines an opportunity that causes people to stretch
The Decision Maker	Makes centralized, abrupt decisions that confuse the organization		The Community Builder	Drives sound decisions by constructing debate and decision-making forums
The Micro Manager	Drives results through their personal involvement		The Investor	Gives other people the ownership for results and invests in their success

THE MIND OF THE MULTIPLIER

As we continued to study both Diminishers and Multipliers, we not only found that they operate in dramatically different ways, we also found that they hold radically different assumptions about the intelligence of the people they work with. If Diminishers see the world of intelligence in black and white, Multipliers see it in Technicolor. Because they think differently, they operate differently, which causes people to respond differently—offering their full intelligence and discretionary energy. The Multiplier mentality is at the source of the 2X Multiplier Effect.

The Multiplier Mindsets

While the Multipliers we studied across education came with different personalities and different strengths in the Multiplier practices, they shared similar mindsets, or assumptions, three in particular.

1. People Are Smart

Multipliers view people as smart and capable; they trust their staff to do hard things and do them well. They see their school or district as full of talented people who are capable of contributing at much higher levels. Instead of wondering if someone is smart, they wonder in what way that person is smart. When Multipliers encounter a problem or challenge, they don't shelter people from it. They expose their team to these challenges assuming, *They are smart and will figure it out*. Sure, they expect people to make mistakes and skin their knees, but they know this is part of the learning process.

2. Intelligence Is Dynamic

Our research confirmed that Multipliers not only access people's current capability, they stretch it. People reported actually getting smarter around Multipliers, implying that intelligence itself can grow. This is an insight corroborated by the growing body of research on the extensible nature of intelligence. Consider two such studies:

- Carol Dweck of Stanford University has conducted groundbreaking research on the effects of a "fixed" mindset verses a "growth" mindset. She's found that when children are given a series of progressively harder puzzles and praised for their intelligence, they plateau for fear of reaching the limit of their intelligence. However, children given the same series of puzzles, but praised instead for their hard work, eagerly take on the challenge of the harder puzzles and increase their ability to reason and solve problems. By exercising their intelligence, they create a belief system, and then a reality, that intelligence grows.[5]

- Eric Turkheimer of the University of Virginia has found that the environment a child is living in can suppress his or her IQ. He and colleagues found that the IQ of the poorest children was almost entirely decided by their socioeconomic status, whereas the environment played a much less significant role for children in the best-off families. In improved environments, children are capable of increasing their intelligence.[6]

3. Curiosity Sparks Intelligence

In our research analyzing traits of multipliers, we found that the most recurrent trait was intellectual curiosity. Multipliers stretch their own minds and the minds of those around them because the question *"why?"* is at the core of their thinking. They wonder what is possible.

With these deeply held beliefs, Multipliers recognize the intelligence in others, provoke it, and cultivate it to its fullest. The leader's own intelligence and curiosity become the catalyst that makes everyone around them smarter and perform at their best.

Consider a high school science teacher and program director with the mind of a Multiplier and a viral, infectious intelligence.

It was a warm July evening in the Santa Cruz Mountains and close to a hundred former "Ridge Rats" gathered to honor their high school science teacher on his 70th birthday. Congregated around a roaring fire, they recounted their time in the Montebello science program with Dan Baer.

Dan, who was only of average build, had an enormous wit that could fill a classroom and a warmth that would light a fire. Dan loved science, but more than that he loved people, especially students. His Ridge program was geared toward the lost and disenfranchised student—he believed in and trusted them. But the program also attracted the smart, college-bound students and even the cool kids—he believed in and trusted them, too. He knew there was a smart kid in every student; his goal was to make them believe in their own intelligence and ability. Dan caught his students by throwing out an observation or two and then reeling them in through their self-led discovery.

Tim Reid, or Timmy as he was called then, was a 14-year-old freshman whose academic life wasn't going well and whose self-esteem was close to nonexistent. He saw no future for himself; his parents saw a son who was floundering with no direction. Having heard of Dan's Ridge program, they secured an interdistrict transfer and enrolled Timmy.

Timmy's journey with Dan started slowly as he and the others followed Dan around like little ducklings. Dan led them through the woods, stopping to investigate the symbiotic relationship between a lizard and its parasite or the wonder and contribution of a spreading oak tree. Dan approached every student differently and guided his or her self-discovery. Soon Timmy (like many others) was convinced he was one of Mr. Baer's favorites. Tim reflected,

> Mr. Baer first figured out what I was good at and then helped me discover it. He knew my talents better than I did. He made me feel like I was intelligent because everything I said he would consider. He made me feel like I was a smart kid and could do something with my life.

Like all the Ridge Rats, Dan pushed them to think and to reach their own conclusions. Tim remembers Mr. Baer once saying, "Nobody discovers anything by giving an answer. You look for the questions. Why? Because good questions lead to big concepts and ideas."

Dan wasn't a red-mark kind of teacher; grades weren't important. But his expectations were extremely high. If Timmy's observations were mediocre, Dan pushed until they were brilliant. He always expected the best from his students. Dan wasn't overbearing; he just expected. With the negative pressure off, Timmy began to blossom.

Timmy entered Dan's Ridge program as a 14-year-old lost soul and left as a high school graduate, realizing that he was intelligent and knowing he had a contribution to make. Timmy became Tim as he entered college and found his academic passion: history. Dan had taught him the value of intellectual inquiry and instilled in him a belief that he could ask deep, intellectual questions and then find answers. Tim graduated from college, entered a PhD program, luckily found another Multiplier in his PhD advisor, and received his doctorate in medical history in two short years. Tim, now Professor Reid, reflected as he gathered around the fire with a hundred other people who were trapped in Dan Baer's sticky web where they caught his contagious intellect. Tim said, "Dan Baer changed my life. I wouldn't be Professor Reid if it weren't for him."

Now on the campus of Oregon State University, Professor Reid gathers his university students and takes them on their own path of discovery. He challenges and pushes their thinking the way Dan did for him years ago.

Dan Baer had an infectious intelligence. He believed that inside each kid was a brilliant mind—a seed trying to push its way up through the soil, find nutrients, and grow. His belief led his students to think a little harder, push themselves a little harder. As another former Ridge Rat, Dr. Eric Allen, said, "Dan taught us how to think, question, discover, and learn. He was always stretching our minds. He made me feel really important. I would have done anything for him."

Dan's beliefs drove his students to work at their best. Perhaps more important, Dan's most deeply held assumptions drove his own behavior, teaching, and leadership style.

Behavior Follows Assumptions

Uncovering and understanding the mindsets of the Multipliers is the key to unlocking the Multiplier Effect. Our assumptions drive our behavior. Our behavior triggers reactions in others, causing them either to step up and operate at their best or to retreat, giving us a fraction of their true capability.

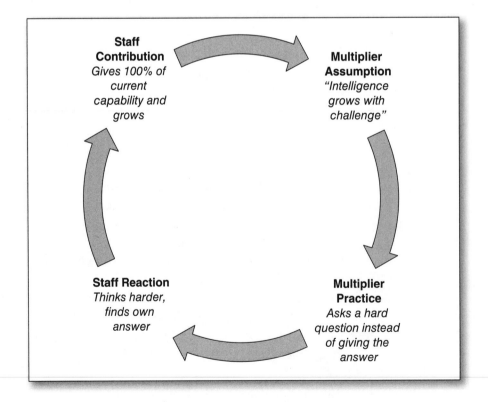

And, unfortunately, when this cycle begins with a Diminisher assumption, it leads to an anemic reaction where people hold back, giving less than half of their capability.

Because our behavior follows our assumptions, often the easiest way to change our behavior is to focus on our assumptions. As Robert Kegan said, "If you want powerful ongoing changes in teaching or leadership, you have to get at the underlying beliefs and conceptions that give rise to behaviors."[7]

How do we learn to see and focus on our own assumptions? Imagine yourself dragged against your better judgment into a Zumba dance exercise class. Your friend explains that it is the hottest cardio fitness craze—Latin dance meets jazzercise. "It will be fun," she says. You are wary, having never tangoed or sambaed and find the limbo challenge enough for you. For Liz this is an all-too-vivid memory.

Once the session begins, the instructor moves smoothly and brilliantly. She makes it look easy. Soon the room is alive with lines of people in the cardio zone and moving in rhythm. Indeed, the scene is pretty hot—but you are most certainly not. You see that your worries are well founded as you move left when everyone moves right. You are shaking, but you don't look a thing like Shakira or really anyone else in the class.

You suffer through, trying to make your arms and legs do what the instructor's are doing. With just 10 minutes left to endure, the instructor sees you in the back and calls to the group, "If you are having a hard time following along, just watch my knees." You think, "Her knees? Her knees are hardly moving. It's the extremities I'm having a hard time keeping up with!" She continues, "Watch my knees. Make your knees do what my knees are doing. The rest of your body will follow." This strikes you as impossible. But you try. You concentrate on the small movement of her knees. Her right knee moves forward and to the left and then back. You mimic the behavior. Your hips starts swinging to the right . . . just like everyone else's. You watch for the next move. Again, your hips swing, your shoulder dips, and soon you find yourself keeping up with the rest of the group, even with some Latin flare. It works. As far as you are concerned, it is a miracle.

"Watch my knees and the rest of your body will follow."

Our *behavior follows our assumptions*, much like our hips follow our knees when we dance. If we want to change the direction of our behavior, we need to change the direction of our assumptions. Sometimes small shifts in our thinking can lead, quite naturally, to significant shifts in our behavior.

What happens when we try to behave like a Multiplier but in our mind we hold some of the assumptions of a Diminisher? If we want to lead like a Multiplier, we need to learn to think like one.

As you read this book, we invite you to reflect on your own assumptions. Do you operate with the belief that *people are smart and will figure this out*? Or do you find yourself in thinking, *they will never figure this out without me*? The chart below summarizes how these very different sets of assumptions have a powerful effect on the way Diminishers and Multipliers lead others.

How would you:	Diminisher *"They will never figure this out without me."*	Multiplier *"People are smart and will figure this out."*
Manage talent?	Use	Develop
Approach mistakes?	Blame	Explore
Set direction?	Tell	Challenge
Make decisions?	Decide	Consult
Get things done?	Control	Support

Often, even a small shift of assumptions can cause us to lead and respond in radically different ways, yielding vastly different performance in the people we lead. For example, instead of wondering how smart your co-leader really is, you might ask, "In what way is he smart?" You will begin to see latent intelligence that may have been hidden below the surface.

Now let's consider the opposite scenario. Suppose you hold the assumptions of Multipliers. You have a growth mindset and see intelligence in abundance; after all, you went into education because you enjoy seeing other people learn and grow. Is it possible to have the mind of a Multiplier but have a diminishing effect? What happens when well-intended leaders follow popular management practices or get so busy they lead without intention? And what happens when they simply replicate what they've seen other leaders do—too many of whom are Diminishers?

THE ACCIDENTAL DIMINISHER

In our research, we were surprised to discover how few Diminishers understood the restrictive impact they were having on others. Most had moved into administration having been praised for their personal, and often intellectual, merit. They assumed their role as leader was to have the answers. Despite our best intentions to be perfect leaders, most of us fall somewhere on the continuum between Amazing Multiplier and Dreadful Diminisher.

The greatest power of these ideas might be in realizing that you have the mind of a Multiplier but that you've been long living in a Diminisher world and you've lost your way. Perhaps you are an Accidental Diminisher. Accidental or not, the impact on your team is the same—you may be harnessing only half of the true brainpower of your team.

How would you know if you are having a diminishing impact despite your best intentions? Perhaps you will see glimmers of your own reflection as you put faces on the Multipliers and Diminishers described throughout the book. The reality is that we all fall somewhere on the Accidental Diminisher scale. Despite our best efforts to be effective leaders, no one is exempt from Accidental Diminisher tendencies: superintendents, directors, managers, site administrators, and teachers. No one. To test the accuracy of your self-reflection, visit MultiplierEffectBook.com to take the 3-minute quiz, "Are You an Accidental Diminisher?" Your quiz score and report will help you consider the ways you might be diminishing others despite your most noble intentions.

THE PROMISE OF THIS BOOK

As we interviewed educators, we heard case after case of smart individuals being underutilized by their leaders. And we heard the pain administrators feel trying to do more with fewer resources or being bound by an overemphasis on standardization and assessment. It is a far-from-perfect world in which our teachers teach and our administrators manage and lead. It is a world filled with roadblocks and frustrations. There truly are more questions than answers in the current world of education. But we also heard from devoted educators committed to finding answers to the field's toughest challenges and intractable problems. It is also a world filled with excitement, challenge, and reward. It is a world in need of leaders who look around and see fields of intelligence, ripe for harvesting. Now is the time for us to utilize all of our intellect.

Multipliers are out there. Multipliers know how to find this dormant intelligence, challenge it, and put it to use at its fullest. Multipliers like those above are more than just geniuses. They are genius makers. They know that at the apex of the intelligence hierarchy is not the lone genius but rather the smart leader who also brings out smarts and capability in everyone around him or her. These leaders exist in business, in education, in nonprofit, and in government.

Consider a few you will learn more about later:

1. Amparo Barrera, a middle school principal who turned a school with a rocky gang reputation into one known for its remarkable academic improvement. People felt stretched

around her, saying, "Amparo knew how to work people almost to their breaking points. I never felt like I was working for her; I was working with her."

2. History teacher Patrick Kelly, who creates an environment that draws out his students' very best thinking and work, and where 95% of his students score at the proficient or advanced levels on state tests.

3. Alyssa Gallagher, an assistant superintendent who is leading a charge to revolutionize learning across the district by giving ownership to the teachers and letting them be the revolutionaries.

4. Jeff Jones, a newly appointed Canadian superintendent who, when faced with massive budget cuts, created forums for discussion and dissent and built popular support across the district for a difficult decision.

5. Larry Gelwix, head coach of Highland Rugby, whose high school varsity team's record is 410 wins and just 10 losses in 35 years. He attributes this extraordinary record to a deliberate leadership philosophy that engages the intelligence of his players on and off the field.

The promise of this book is simple: You can be a Multiplier. You can create genius around you and receive a higher contribution from your people. You can choose to think like a Multiplier and operate like one. This book will show you how. And it will also show you why it matters.

This book is for principals and assistant principals who are mired in the random chaos of the job, who feel like air traffic controllers, who wonder when they will find the time to be the leader they envisioned. It's for our superintendents and their cabinets who must find the balance between needs and resources while managing change and keeping their schools running. It is for our teachers who welcome and teach whomever they get, who are underrecognized and underappreciated. It's for all the hardworking administrators, educators, and teacher leaders out there in our small towns and our big cities holding the future of our nation on their shoulders.

This is a book for every educational leader trying to navigate the resource strain of tough economic times. It is a message for leaders who must accomplish more by getting more out of their people. As our schools face dwindling resources, the need for leaders who can multiply the intelligence and capability around them is more vital than ever.

This book is for the raging Multiplier who seeks to better understand what he or she does naturally. It is for the aspiring Multiplier who wishes to get the full capability and intelligence from his or her people. And it is most certainly for the Accidental Diminisher that resides in each of us. This is a book for all of our educators. It's for the Multipliers of the present and those who will yet become Multipliers.

As you read this book, you will find a few central messages:

1. Diminishers underutilize people and leave capability on the table.

2. Multipliers increase intelligence in people and in organizations. People actually get smarter and more capable around them. Great educators do this instinctively, sending students home every day knowing that they have been challenged and they are smart. Educational leaders who are Multipliers extend that same logic and conviction to their colleagues.

3. Multipliers leverage their resources. School systems can get 2X more from their resources by turning their most intelligent resources into intelligence Multipliers.

This book is a framework to help you develop the practices of a Multiplier. The following chapters will clarify the differences between Multipliers and Diminishers and will present the five disciplines of the Multiplier. You will read stories of real Multipliers and Diminishers; be aware that we've changed the Diminishers' names (and schools) for rather obvious reasons. The book concludes with a road map for becoming a Multiplier and creating a Multiplier school.

As you are reading this book, you may be tempted to lay the template of change on the Diminishers in your life. You may want to say, "Ahh, how sweet it would be if Bill would start leading like a Multiplier. How much better *my* life would be." Resist the temptation. The biggest change you can make, actually the only change you can make, is to yourself. Enjoy the journey. Begin with a step.

Let us now introduce you to the fascinating and diverse set of leaders we call the Multipliers. They come from all walks of life—from our schools' administrative offices to our schools' classrooms, from corporate boardrooms to the office cubicle. We've selected leaders and educators who represent diverse ideologies, backgrounds, and experiences. We encourage you to learn from everyone. We hope you will find their stories, their practices, and their impact as inspiring as we did when we entered their worlds.

End Notes

1. Name of leader has been changed.

2. Name of leader has been changed.

3. Paul Ainsworth, "Getting the Most from Your Staff," *Secondary Headship* (December 2010/January 2011).

4. Carmen DeNavas-Walt, Bernadette D. Proctor, and Jessica C. Smith, *Income, Poverty and Health Insurance Coverage in the United States: 2010.* http://www.census .gov/prod/2011pubs/p60-239.pdf

5. Carol Dweck, *Mindset: The New Psychology of Success* (New York: Random House, 2006).

6. David L. Kirp, "After the Bell Curve," *New York Times*, July 23, 2006.

7. Dennis Sparks, "Inner conflicts, inner strengths: An interview with Robert Kegan and Lisa Lahey," *Journal of Staff Development 23*, no. 3 (2000).

At A Glance: The Multiplier Effect

THE MODEL

DIMINISHERS	MULTIPLIERS
These leaders are absorbed in their own intelligence, stifle others, and deplete the organization of crucial intelligence and capability.	These leaders are genius makers and bring out the intelligence in others. They build collective, viral intelligence in organizations.
SEE	**SEE**
The Assumption "People won't figure it out without me"	**The Assumption** "People are smart and will figure it out"
DO	**DO**
The Five Disciplines of the Diminisher	**The Five Disciplines of the Multiplier**
The Gate Keeper Hoards resources and underutilizes talent	**The Talent Finder** Attracts talented people & uses them at their highest point of contribution
The Tyrant Creates a tense environment that suppresses people's thinking and capability	**The Liberator** Creates an intense environment that requires people's best thinking and work
The Know-It-All Gives directives that showcase how much they know	**The Challenger** Defines an opportunity that causes people to stretch
The Decision Maker Makes centralized, abrupt decisions that confuse the organization	**The Community Builder** Drives sound decisions by constructing decision-making forums
The Micromanager Drives results through their personal involvement	**The Investor** Gives other people ownership for results and invests in their success
GET	**GET**
The Result 40%	**The Result** 2.3X

2

The Talent Finder

Life is like a ten speed bicycle. Most of us have gears we never use.

Charles M. Schultz

Russell Dow, a graduate student in geology at the Colorado School of Mines, sat studying satellite images and aerial photos of the Arizaro deposit in Argentina. For his master's thesis, Dow was mapping the eroded volcanic edifice where this mineral deposit owned by Mansfield Mines sat. While studying the maps, he noticed a steep cone-shaped hill on the edge of the map. This unchartered outcropping had a distinct white halo, often a sign of thermal activity. Dow made a mental note to check out this area during his upcoming visit. Months later, 14,700 feet high in the Andes, he charges up the slope, headed for the steep cone. As he ascends, he notices interesting bits of rock—malachite, quartz, and magnetite. He climbs until he sees an exposed area, revealing rich mineral deposits below. Russell's discovery prompts Mansfield Minerals to investigate further, drilling 130 exploratory holes in the now-called Lindero deposit and conducting a deeper study revealing a viable mine, rich in natural deposits.[1] Dow's finder's fee should do nicely to pay back his student loans!

Like minerals, talent needs to be discovered and then mined. To find it, leaders need to get "coal faced" or close to the source so they can see it, understand it deeply, and know how to extract and use it fully. But, unlike natural resources, reservoirs of talent don't deplete with extraction—they grow with use.

Some leaders know how to dig deep to unearth and extract the unique and native genius of people around them. Other leaders wall it off. This chapter explores these two approaches to the management of talent and why one creates a cycle of accelerated growth and the other a cycle of decline.

THE GATEKEEPER VERSUS THE TALENT FINDER

Multipliers operate as Talent Finders, identifying genius in the people around them and then using this genius to its fullest. You might think of it as working at their highest point of contribution. People contribute more and grow faster.

In contrast, Diminishers operate as Gatekeepers who are overly protective of people and the status quo. They treat people like resources, pigeon holing them and limiting their visibility and growth. They are more likely to label someone's performance than they are to put a name to someone's unique genius. For them, resources are to be curated and horded. Around Gatekeepers, people are collected like knickknacks in grandma's curio cabinet—on display for everyone to see, but not well utilized.

Defending the Status Quo

Willow Oaks School District[2] is one of those districts that real estate agents like to tout to prospective buyers fortunate enough to move into the district. Blessed with an achieving student population in an affluent community, it has a stellar reputation and is known for its progressive practices. But tucked inside this district is Sinclair Middle School, with the challenges of a large English language learner and special education population.

The new superintendent, Harold Tang,[3] quickly sizes up the situation and figures out that Sinclair and its disadvantaged population is a potential liability for the district's high profile. His strategy is simple: Box it off and ignore it. Harold's interactions with Daniel, Sinclair's principal, are superficial, while he spends his time with his elite, favorite schools.

Meanwhile, Daniel and his team revamp service delivery to special education students, adopting a leading-edge approach and a true paradigm shift. Soon the entire staff of Sinclair is on board and implementing the program and experiencing the buds of success.

Daniel is eager to share their success with the rest of the district, but he isn't allowed direct communication with the superintendent. Instead he works through Harold's go-between. He doesn't even feel like a legitimate member of the superintendent's cabinet. It appears that the superintendent is protecting the other schools from Sinclair's infamy.

The Sinclair team continues to make progress, but the rest of the district largely ignores their innovative work. The team figures out quickly that they have limited support for their work and aren't expected to think beyond the status quo. Daniel accepts a position at another school, taking his progressive thinking with him. Despite the reality of its successes, Sinclair's reputation declines, leaving as wide of a gap as ever within the rest of the district.

The superintendent didn't look deep enough to see that he had a dynamic site principal in his most challenging school. Instead he boxed him in and labeled him, based on school reputation, as not useful, thereby shutting down intelligence and innovative thinking throughout an entire school.

Are there people on your team that you've sized up, boxed in, and labeled? Perhaps you're overlooking latent intelligence. The best leaders don't shut people in boxes; they put their talent on display.

Fit for a Race

In 2010, the senior leaders of the Eastern Carver County School District, in the Twin Cities area of Minnesota, gathered to learn how to be Multipliers. Intrigued by the ideas, Dana Kauzlarich Miller and Jay Woller, the principal and assistant principal of Pioneer Ridge Middle School, in Chaska, decided to introduce the ideas to their leadership council.

As soon as the new school year got underway, they held their first staff meeting to explore how to be better Multipliers across their school. After initial exploration, Dana and Jay gave each teacher a survey that included the question, "How can we tap into each person's talent at our school?" Megan, a relatively new physical education teacher, wanted to better understand this question, so she dropped by to see Dana and Jay. This sparked a conversation about her passion for fitness and her concerns for childhood obesity in the community. Megan offered an idea—maybe the school could sponsor a 5K race for the entire Chaska community. Dana was delighted at the idea and urged Megan to take the lead. Megan was at first reluctant, reflecting on her workload as a new teacher who was enrolled in a master's program, but she was drawn to it. She took the lead and ran with it. Other teachers and staff joined in, freely sharing their skills by volunteering their technology expertise and by designing t-shirts, posters, and banners. The school technology teacher even had her mini-classes researching 5K races.

As the planning ensued, it became clear that this event could serve as both a community-building event and a much-needed fundraiser for their building/technology fund. With this heightened goal, Megan's heart raced just a bit. While she had a knack for organization, she had never organized an activity on this scale. Megan poured herself into the effort, devoting time and energy. Even with her workload, Megan never looked exhausted. In fact, her colleagues said she looked exhilarated. She was racing forward, not stuck in a rut.

With Megan's passion fueling their work, the team held a spectacular race, supported and attended by over 90% of the staff and received with accolades from the community. Not only did 300 children and adults run the 5K distance, but the school raised $7,000, enough money to upgrade the school's technology and fund next year's race.

By tapping into the native genius and passions of the staff, this administrative team unlocked latent capability and discretionary effort across the entire school. How fully are you using the talent of your team? Unlock talent and let it run.

A Cycle of Attraction

Under the leadership of the Talent Finder, the genius of people gets discovered and utilized to the fullest. Having been stretched, these players become smarter and more capable. A players become A+ players. These people are positioned in the spotlight and get kudos and recognition for their work. They attract attention, and their reputation grows. These A+ players get offered even bigger opportunities and seize them with the full support of the Talent Finder.

The cycle then kicks into hyper drive. As this pattern of utilization, growth, and opportunity occurs across multiple levels, others notice. The administrator, the school, or the district gets a reputation. It builds a reputation as a "place to grow." This reputation spreads, and more A players flock to work in the leaders' organization. So there is a steady flow of talent in the door, replacing any talent that might grow out of the organization.

A CYCLE OF ATTRACTION

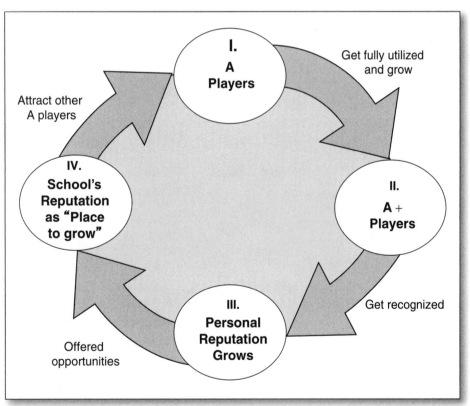

A Cycle of Decline

Around Gatekeepers, the real genius of people gets overlooked and boxed in. The A players have limited impact and start to look more like A– or B+. They fail to get noticed for their work, and they lose intellectual confidence. They begin to recede into the shadow of the Gatekeeper. Their reputation suffers and opportunities evaporate. So they stay and wait, hoping things will turn around. But as they wait around for a change in leadership, their confidence wanes. They "fight" until they have no more energy and eventually utilize their skills in other areas of their life where their contributions are valued. They roam the halls as the walking dead. On the outside these zombies go through the motions, but on the inside they have given up. They "quit and stay" and take a seat at the table in the staff room where those that are "past their sell-by date" gather.

Unfortunately, this cycle of degeneration can impact more than one person; it can infect an entire school.

A CYCLE OF DECLINE

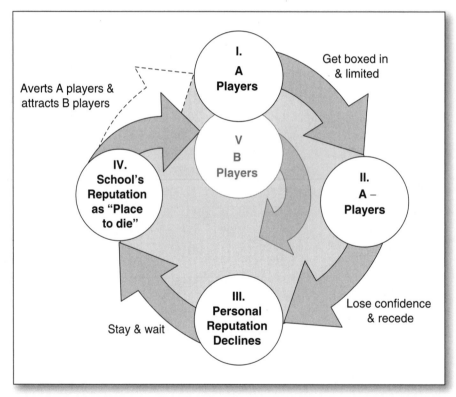

THE TALENT FINDER

Talent Finders see genius all around them. They see it and they put it to use, stretching and strengthening the talent. People can't help but grow around them. These leaders see talent in others because they are oriented outward, focused on other people, seeing each person as a unique treasure waiting to be discovered.

The Mind of the Multiplier

Multipliers hold a deep belief that intelligence exists in abundance. They believe that everyone has talent and intelligence and something to contribute. They see intelligence in high definition.

While everyone has something to contribute, not everyone is contributing at the same level. Multipliers see talent less like an industrial park (a sprawling collection of near identical three-story buildings) and more like a city skyline. Imagine the San Francisco skyline on a sunny day. It's a striking composition of silhouettes, each building at a different height. Some stand at 8 stories while the tallest rises 48 stories. Some are composed of gray or white stone, a few are brick, and many combine cement and green-tinted glass. And, of course, there are a few iconic structures such as the Transamerica Building, with its triangular slopes. As with most skylines, its beauty stems from its jutted, irregular profile.

To Multipliers, people are such skylines. They appreciate the rich diversity of intelligence and talent around them. They acknowledge that not everyone is at the same level of capability, but they believe that everyone's capability can increase. Instead of trying to bring everyone to the same level, they level-up each person, building a floor or two of capacity at a time. A great educator does the same in a classroom or in a school.

With these assumptions, a Talent Finder can find genius in everyone. Sure, it is rewarding to lead a team comprised solely of A players and superstars, but rarely do administrators get to assemble a fresh team. Most educational leaders need to optimize the hand that they've been dealt.

Cami Anderson, superintendent of the Newark school system, exemplifies this mindset. She is a devoted educator who believes that all children are capable of achieving at the highest level regardless of their circumstances. Newark mayor Cory Booker said of her,

> Cami declared that whether a child has been incarcerated or pregnant or had dropped out, aged out or flunked out, she could still nurture her genius, learn, develop, and yes, graduate. She is determined to end a long local and national nightmare in which too many of our children are casualties of our failure to serve their genius.[4]

THE THREE PRACTICES OF THE TALENT FINDER

Talent Finders look for talent everywhere and in everyone, then study that talent to uncover and unlock the real genius that lies within.

How does a Talent Finder unlock this genius and build new capability? In our research studying Multipliers in educational settings, we found three consistent practices: (1) scout out diverse intelligence, (2) find people's native genius, and (3) utilize people at their fullest.

1. Scout Out Diverse Intelligence

Value Multiple Intelligences

In 1904, Alfred Binet created an intelligence evaluation method that would eventually become the IQ test.[5] Unfortunately, it has developed into a means of labeling people as either natively smart or natively deficient. Counteracting this misuse of the IQ test, researchers such as Daniel Goleman and Carol Dweck have spent the past two decades seeking better means of identifying and understanding intelligence. The message from this new body of research is clear: Our capabilities extend far beyond what a simple IQ score says.

A Talent Finder knows that genius comes in many forms and that intelligence has many facets. A Talent Finder is able to identify the particular types of genius that are present in each person around him or her and then help those geniuses thrive.

Scout Talent

Talent Finders not only value the diversity of talent in front of them, they find ways to bring top talent into their teams. And often they don't have to actively scout this talent. Talent Finders gain access to the best talent, not because they are necessarily great recruiters, but rather because people are drawn to work for them.

Dedee Rodriquez was on a mission to transform Willow Glen Middle School, a neglected school struggling to find its own identity in San Jose, California. As the associate principal, she was an underling of the co-joined high school, but she had big plans to return the middle school to its former status. Dedee, known for appreciating the talent of her teachers and using it fully, had soon built a stellar reputation among teachers and other administrators.

Dedee had several teaching vacancies and knew that she wanted to fill them with superstar teachers. She had hopes of attracting some of the best teachers in the district, but as all principals know, there is an unwritten ethic between principals—no stealing teachers away from your colleagues. So recruiting teachers was out of the question.

With a little ingenuity, Dedee attracted some of the best teachers in the district without contacting a single one. How'd she do it? She gathered her teacher leaders and asked a simple question, "Do you know any stellar teachers who would like to work here?" This sparked action, and Willow Glen's teachers eagerly reached out to their colleagues with the invitation, "How would you like to work for Dedee?" New teachers, not able to resist the carrot, joined the school, filling the available openings and other new openings as they became available. This influx of A-level talent strengthened the school, its reputation, and its culture of valuing and growing talent.

To know Dedee was to want to work for her. To work for her was to want to stay with her. Her reputation did the recruiting. Do you shoulder the burden of recruiting great talent, or does the culture of your school do the recruiting for you?

When leaders value talent, it is easy to recruit top talent.

Andy Garrido, a seasoned principal in Cupertino School District, was one of those talent-seeking Multipliers. He was constantly scouting for talent; he believed smart people could accomplish great things, as Jennifer West, a Stanford graduate with a master's degree in communication, can attest. The year was 2000 and Jennifer was working as a noncredentialed PE specialist at Dilworth School, where Andy was serving as interim principal. She was leading a PE activity and noticed "the principal" watching her. Just having him watch her made her nervous. When he approached her and told her he needed to see her in his office, nervous was elevated to a new level. Jennifer's heart was pounding as she walked into Andy's office to be greeted by "What are you doing? . . ." All Jennifer could think of was "What have I done wrong?" Andy's greeting continued with "You are wasting your God-given talent. You are meant to teach. Now, this is what you are going to do. You are going to enroll in a credential intern program at Santa Clara University *this* summer. You *are* going to get your credential. You *will* become a teacher." Jennifer did! And she has been teaching ever since—grateful to Andy Garrido for naming her genius.

Andy innately saw capacity in people whether they recognized it or not. He then gave them the tools, and sometimes a nudge, to become successful.

2. Find People's Native Genius

As an engineer for Cummins Inc. Elise worked with a wide cross-section of junior engineers, often interacting with many new hires and summer interns. It was almost inevitable that at some point during their assignment, junior engineers would approach her asking for advice on how to navigate a career path in such a large organization. Elise would readily jump in, making connections and pointing them in the right direction. She enjoyed doing this and always found the time, but Elise wondered:

> Why am I always the one who gets asked to make connections for these new hires? After seeing this pattern repeated over many years at work and in the community, I realized that I wasn't being asked to make introductions per se; I was helping people navigate. One particular colleague, Elma, explained it to me: "It is because you see the bigger picture and can connect the dots." What? I stared at her blankly, trying to decipher what she was saying. It sounded like she was telling me that I was good at breathing. It didn't strike me as a particularly big deal or something someone else might find difficult. What my colleagues were teaching me was that I had a native ability for making connections, something that I did both easily and freely.

Identify It

Talent Finders know how to uncover and access the native genius of others. By *native genius* we mean something even more specific than a strength or a skill that might be highly rated on an assessment. Native genius is something that people not only do exceptionally well, but absolutely naturally. They do it easily and freely.

What people do easily, they do without conscious effort. They do it better than anything else they do, but they don't need to apply extraordinary effort to the task. They get results that are head and shoulders above others without breaking a sweat.

What people do freely, they do without condition. They don't need to be paid or rewarded, and they often don't even need to be asked. It is something that gives them inherent satisfaction, and they offer their capability voluntarily, even ardently. It is effortless, and they stand ready and willing to contribute, whether it is a formal job requirement or not. It is what they can't help but do; it is what they were built to do.

Finding someone's native genius is the key that unlocks discretionary effort. It propels people to go beyond what is required and offer their full intelligence. Finding people's genius begins by carefully observing them in action, looking for spikes of authentic enthusiasm and natural flow of energy. As you watch someone in action, ask these questions:

- What do they do better than anything else they do?
- What do they do better than the people around them?
- What do they do without effort?
- What do they do without being asked?
- What do they do readily without being paid?

Rosie McColl had always been an inspirational English teacher at the Berkhamsted School, in Hertfordshire, England, but her native genius didn't reveal itself fully until she started harnessing web-based technologies in her teaching of literature and creative writing. She would dig into a new technology, often working late into the evenings and on weekends, until she discovered an innovative way to teach English. For example, she discovered a way to use Google Docs to encourage her students to collaboratively share their ideas about *The Great Gatsby* with the other students rather than just taking notes in class or on their own. The process not only resulted in a significantly higher volume of work but allowed students to engage deeper and take greater ownership of their learning. And just as soon as the new tools proved successful with her students, she shared the ideas with the rest of the department. Mark Steed, the principal of Berkhamsted, noticed Rosie's penchant for technology and created a role in the e-learning team with schoolwide responsibility enabling her to implement these innovations with 200 teachers and make a difference across the entire 1,500-person student body.

Rosie, just 3 months into her new assignment, said, "I'm fortunate to have my combined interest in collaborative learning and new technologies recognized and to have the freedom to further develop my skills in this area. I'm enjoying seeing a similar enthusiasm sparked in colleagues." This inspirational English teacher not only inspired her students, she was able to use her native genius to inspire innovative teaching across the entire school.

Label It

Native genius can be so instinctive for people that they may not even understand their own capability; after all, "fish discover water last." But if people aren't aware of their genius, they are not in a position to deliberately utilize it. By telling people what you see, you can raise their awareness and confidence, allowing them to provide their capability more fully.

Players for Larry Gelwix, head coach of the almost unbeatable Highland High School rugby team, often report that he got more out of them than other coaches. For one player, John, this meant Larry publicly noting what a fast runner he was. John said of the experience, "Being told I had speed inspired me to develop a distinct self-concept: I was fast. And every time I found myself in a situation where speed was required, I remembered this, and I pushed myself beyond my limits." It was important for Larry verbally to recognize John's native genius because speed was so natural to John that he didn't even notice it. Finding people's native genius and then labeling it is a direct approach to drawing more intelligence from them.

Talent Finders appreciate the myriad forms that intelligence comes in. They look for talent everywhere and in everyone and then study that talent to uncover and unlock the real genius that lies within. Like Dana and Jay at Pioneer Ridge Middle School, they look for the native genius of each member of the team. And when they find it, they name it: "Megan Williams has a passion for fitness and the community. She'll be organizing a 5K race for the Pioneer Ridge Middle School community!"

3. Utilize People at Their Fullest

When Talent Finders discover someone's native genius, they've earned the right to put him or her to work. They're not on a power trip; they're intent on injecting valuable brainpower and energy into the organization while also offering a rich and rewarding experience for the individual. The idea is simple. People love to contribute their genius. When a leader figures out someone's true genius, the leader has opened up a pathway for that person to contribute, and contribute in the most meaningful way.

Find Their Highest Point of Contribution

Courtney Cadwell was a seventh-grade math teacher in her first year of teaching at Egan Junior High School in the Los Altos School District. She's had a deep and true love of math and science, but also a penchant for innovation and a drive to experiment with new ideas. What would a typical administrator do with Courtney? Make sure she was happy? Move her to a higher grade level or give her the honors classes? Such actions would surely signal her value to the school and energize her as a teacher.

But Courtney's appetite for classroom experimentation and innovation caught the attention of her principal, who had been asked to recommend a teacher to pilot a blended learning solution that would integrate the Khan Academy. You see, the district had established a bold vision to revolutionize learning for all students, and the assistant superintendent, Alyssa Gallagher, was assembling a pilot team.

These four teachers, each passionate about rethinking math instruction, jumped in. As they developed new approaches to deeply integrate technology and online learning into their curriculum, they encountered many obstacles and some messy gray areas. Courtney stepped in asking questions, exploring options, and helping others make sense of the complexity. Alyssa noticed how these messy areas seem to bring out Courtney's natural leadership. But why? Alyssa watched her closely, noting that Courtney had a genius for navigating complexity. Somehow, the grayer the issues, the better Courtney was.

After completing a wildly successful pilot, Alyssa wrangled the funding to take the new blended learning instructional strategies to the next level and spread these practices across all upper grade math classes involving over 50 teachers. She tapped Courtney to be the district math coach, spending half of her time in her own classroom and the other half guiding the other teachers' ability to implement technology in their classrooms. As these teachers encountered obstacles, Courtney helped them navigate as well. When a teacher couldn't see how to do it without a computer for each student, Courtney asked what could be done with just five computers. Soon they found a way to rotate students. With Courtney's coaching, teachers turned their questions into next steps until the new blended learning strategies were evident in classrooms across the entire district.

By year three, the passion to innovate had become infectious across the school. The parent community took notice and eagerly supplied additional funding for three full-time coaching roles that included a technology integration coach, an innovative strategies coach, and a STEM (science, technology, engineering, math) coach. With Courtney serving as the full-time STEM coach, she was now able to influence all teachers in rethinking instructional practices not only in math but also in science. There was so much interest in the innovation this team was driving, Alyssa organized open house events for other school leaders to come and learn how they could create blended learning environments to revolutionize learning for their students. And when they came, they had Courtney there helping them navigate the gray areas.

When leaders connect people's natural passions and native genius to big opportunities, those people are used at their highest point of contribution. For Alyssa, this wasn't a lucky discovery; it was a deliberate management approach. She studied Courtney, as well as each of the other team members, noticing what each of them did naturally and freely. She then put them to work at their fullest, tackling the district's aspiration to revolutionize learning for all students.

Are there people on your team who could lead a revolution if they were unleashed on the right opportunity? Are there people on your team who aren't being used at their highest?

Shine a Spotlight

Each summer in the Sierra Mountains of California, roughly 75 teenage girls eagerly gather for an annual girls' camp—a week of fun, adventure, and camaraderie that often serves as a watershed event in their young lives. The camp is run entirely on the volunteer efforts of 60 leaders. For the last 6 years, Marguerite Hancock has served (also as a volunteer) as the camp director at the helm of this incredible group of youth and leaders.

Marguerite works as a Stanford University teacher and researcher and is smart, accomplished, and extraordinarily capable. She is a strong leader with strong ideas of her own. One of her assistant directors said, "Marguerite is so capable, she could do virtually any aspect of girls' camp herself." But what is interesting about Marguerite isn't that she could—it is that she *doesn't*. Instead, she leads like a Multiplier, invoking brilliance and dedication in the other 59 leaders who make this camp a reality.

Marguerite begins by building a "dream team" carefully recruited for each person's individual strengths. One of the assistant directors said, "Marguerite studies people. She watches them until she figures out what they are great at. She chose her assistant directors not only for their strengths but because we had strengths in areas where she was weak." She then finds a place where each person's strengths will shine. For some, it is working with the girls one-on-one; for another, it is managing the sports program; for another is it leading the nightly campfire. But each role is carefully cast to draw upon the unique talents of every person on the team.

Marguerite then makes it clear to each person why he or she has been selected for that role. She not only notices their talent; she labels it for them. One camp leader said, "She tells me the talent she sees in me and why it matters. She tells me why girls' camp will be better because of me and my work." But Marguerite doesn't stop there. She lets everyone else know, too. It is typical for her to introduce someone to the group by saying, "This is Jennifer. She's a creative genius, and we are so fortunate to have her on our team."

With her cast of talent assembled, Marguerite then goes to the back of the room, takes control of the spotlight, and begins shining it on others. She is effusive with praise, but it is never empty. Her praise of others' work is specific, and it is public. The other leaders at camp can see the direct link between their work and the success of camp. A camp leader said, "She not only tells you that you are doing a great job, but she tells you why it matters to these girls. I know my work is appreciated."

Marguerite finds other people's genius and then shines a spotlight on it for everyone to see their talent in action. What is the result? A character-building, life-changing experience for 75 young women, but also a deeply rewarding, growing experience for the 59 leaders who serve along with Marguerite.

Working for a Talent Finder offers a thrilling ride, one where people are appreciated for their greatness and then fully utilized, stretched and made ready for the next big challenge. Working with a Gatekeeper holds a very different promise, one fraught with politics, protectionism, and limitations.

THE DIMINISHERS' APPROACH TO MANAGING TALENT

Protect. Control. Limit. This is the mentality of the Gatekeeper. According to Wikipedia, a gatekeeper is a person who controls access to something, for example, via a city gate. In the late 20th century the term came into metaphorical use, referring to individuals who decide whether a given message will be distributed by a mass medium. When it comes to managing talent, Diminishers take the role of the Gatekeeper: They preserve order and keep people where they are, limiting their visibility and their professional growth.

Put People in Boxes

In education, it's not uncommon to label students; you frequently hear terms like *lazy, unmotivated,* and *behavior problem,* among others.

The famous "Pygmalion" study by Rosenthal and Jacobson (1968) demonstrated the critical influence expectations play on outcomes; they found when teachers were led to expect superior results from children, indeed the children would deliver on these results.[6] Diminisher school leaders have a tendency to do the same with their staff; for example, once a special educator, always a special educator. How do your expectations influence the performance you see in your faculty and staff? Are you putting your staff in a box they have no hope of escaping? Or are you giving them light so you can watch them blossom?

Maintain the Status Quo

While Multipliers call out the unique talents and contributions of individuals on their team, Diminishers tend to gloss over these important distinctions and treat people en masse.

When Justin, a sixth-grade core teacher at a high-performing middle school, received a prestigious teaching award, he shared the good news with one of his colleagues. Thrilled for him, the fellow teacher approached the school's principal suggesting she announce it in their next staff meeting and to the community. The principal refused, saying she wouldn't call attention to any specific teacher because they were a team and all deserved equal attention. Sadly, Justin called the newspaper himself. Other teachers got word of Justin's accomplishment and knew that extraordinary performance on their part wasn't likely to get honored either.

When leaders fail to recognize the talents and contributions of individuals, it spawns mediocrity and encourages performance at the average or lowest common denominator. Truly, the best teams are collections of brilliantly unique contributors, not a pool of homogenous, fungible assets. Professor J. Bonner Ritchie was taught an important lesson by one of his students at the University of Michigan during the civil rights movement. She told him, "You are good at treating everyone as equals, but you don't recognize our differences and what makes us unique (e.g., as a woman or an African American growing up in Detroit). In order to treat people equally you have to treat them differently." When a team celebrates the accomplishments of each member, it strengthens the individual and the entire team.

Protect People and Control Resources

Not only did the above principal of the high-performing middle school not want to spotlight any one teacher's successes, she also didn't want to let the spotlight shine on lower performers either. When faced with a mandate to implement rigorous staff evaluations, she spread her wings to protect the staff and then dragged her feet to implement the evaluations. In the meantime, she actively told the staff not to worry because she would just give everyone a default "satisfactory" on their evaluations. Her intent may have been to unify the team, but her protective instincts probably just protected the status quo.

As Diminishers play the role of Gatekeeper, they maintain control and order. But in defending the status quo, ironically, they don't preserve it. They operate in a "one brain, many hands" model of leadership, which stunts the growth of intelligence and talent around them. People around them atrophy. As talent languishes, so does the ambition of the organization. Organizations run by Diminishers too often are elephant graveyards where talent goes to die.

BECOMING A TALENT FINDER

How do you create this cycle of growth and acceleration inside your organization? You can learn to be a genius watcher and spot the native genius of everyone around you. Imagine, if you will, a new high school principal learning to "genius watch," quietly observing each member of his team noticing what they did naturally and freely. Having practiced for 2 weeks, he found how easy it was to spot genius—everywhere.

The new genius watcher takes his regular seat at the county office of education conference room for this month's meeting of the Curriculum Leadership Council. The scene is the same: same chairs, same table, same eight people, and actually the same investigative topic.

What's new is his new genius discovery attitude driving the way he views his fellow committee members. As he watches, he is particularly occupied with Ellen, a curriculum coach from a rival high school. First, he notices her thoughtfully prepared analysis of the reading assignment. When the discussion turns to developing an implementation timeline, it is Ellen who sees the pitfalls of an early adoption. He thinks, "Right on." Because he is looking for genius, he notices Ellen's genius for critical thinking for the first time. He found himself asking, "If she worked at my site, how could I best use her genius?" He left the meeting suspecting that he had staff members, like Ellen, whose native genius he had overlooked, and he was determined to become adept at seeing, naming, and using the genius of everyone around him.

You can get started as a Talent Finder with either of the following two experiments. The experiments you'll find throughout this book are designed to help you take the first few steps in incorporating the Multiplier practices in your own leadership. Each offers a brief description of the experiment, the practices, the mindsets needed to make these practices authentic, and a few caveats to guide your learning. Each experiment offers a template to plan, capture, and reflect on your learning.

Multiplier Experiments

1. **Name the Genius**—You might kick-start this cycle by tapping into someone's native genius and unlocking hidden reserves of discretionary effort. You can start by finding the native genius (that which they do easily and freely) of each individual on your team. Or you might be selective and focus on an individual you are struggling to work with or understand how to utilize. Perhaps this is the person you wish you could remove from the team. Instead of asking, "Is this person smart?" you might ask, "In what way is this person smart?" Once you have some practice identifying native genius (in both yourself and others), you can conduct this exercise as an entire management team so that each team member understands the native genius of each person on the team.

2. **SuperSize It**—You might try sizing someone's job the way you shop for shoes for a young child. How do wise parents decide what size to buy? They might start by measuring the child's foot, but then they buy the pair that's a size too big. And how do the parents respond when their child tries on those shoes, awkwardly parading down the store isle, and declares, "These shoes feel weird. My feet are flopping around in them. They are too big." The parents reassure the child, "Don't worry, you'll grow into them."

   Try supersizing someone's job at your school site. Assess the person's current capabilities and then give him or her a challenge that is a size too big. Give a teacher a leadership role; give an assistant principal more decision-making power. If they seem startled, acknowledge that the role or responsibility might feel awkward at first. Then step back and watch them grow into it.

Multiplier Experiments

Name The Genius

Identify the native genius of each person on your team.

Find the native genius of individuals on your team and find novel ways to utilize their genius more fully. Do this individually or as a team so that everyone understands the native genius of each person on the team.

Multiplier Discipline: **Talent Finder**, remedy for "Org Manager" Accidental Diminisher

Multiplier Mindset:

Everyone is brilliant at something.

Multiplier Practices:

For individuals:

1. Identify it: the things that this person does natively. Ask:
    - What do they do better than anything else they do?
    - What do they do better than the people around them?
    - What do they do *easily* (without effort or even awareness)?
    - What do they do *freely* (without being asked or being paid)?

2. Label it: Give their native genius a short name (e.g., "Synthesizing complex ideas" or "Building bridges" or "Identifying root causes") Test your hypothesis with the person's colleagues and with the person. Refine it until it captures their genius.

3. Work it: Identify roles or tasks that will utilize and extend this person's genius. Go beyond formal jobs and identify ad hoc roles. Have a conversation with the individual and allow them to identify the best ways to utilize their genius.

Across an entire team:

1. Define the concept of native genius (see above)

2. Ask each person to identify the native genius of each colleague

3. Bring the group together

4. Focus on one individual at a time
    a. Have each team member describe that person's native genius
    b. Ask the person to offer their own perspective
    c. Discuss ways to best utilize this person's genius

Caveat: You might find it easier to identify and name your own genius before asking others to do it.

The Promise:

Finding someone's native genius is the key that unlocks discretionary effort. When you tap into native genius people go beyond what is required and offer their full intelligence. When a team understands the native genius of each member, they collaborate more readily and easily.

(Continued)

(Continued)

Use this worksheet to plan and reflect on your Multiplier Experiments.

1. Experiment Purpose

What problem are you trying to address?	What do you hope to accomplish?

2. Document Your Plan

When and where will you try this?	What might limit success?	What will you do to overcome these hurdles?

3. Establish Measures

How will you know if you've been successful?	How will you get feedback?

4. Evaluate Results

What happened?	What impact did you have on others?	What was accomplished?

5. Study Your Learning

What surprised you?	What could you do differently to improve your results?	How would you describe the return on your investment for this experiment?

6. Make Lasting Change

How will you make this part of your on-going management practice?	When and where will you use this approach again?

We'd love to hear about your successes with this Multiplier Experiment. Visit MultiplierEffectBook.com to share your story.

Multiplier Experiments

SuperSize It

Give someone a job that is a size too big.

Acknowledge that everyone on your team is at different capability levels. But everyone is capable of growth. Carve out roles and responsibilities the way you shop for shoes for preschoolers . . . one size too big. And then let the person grow into their new responsibilities.

Multiplier Discipline: **Talent Finder, Challenger, Investor**, remedy for "Org Manager" Accidental Diminisher

---

Multiplier Mindset:

Everyone can grow.

Multiplier Practices:

1. Map out the capability levels of your team, acknowledging that they will probably look more like a jagged skyline than a high-jump bar.

2. Pick one or two people who are ready for a stretch.

3. Map out a set of responsibilities that are beyond their current capabilities that will cause them to really stretch. Let them know you are giving them "a job" that might feel a bit too big. Affirm your belief in their ability to learn and grow into the role.

4. Maintain a vacuum that must be filled . . . by them, not you.

5. Do the same across all the individuals on your team.

Caveat: Give harder work, not more work. Doing more of the same thing doesn't grow our capabilities (unless we are knife jugglers).

The Promise:

People and organizations stretch when there is a healthy gap between what needs to be done and what the current capabilities of the individuals or team are. When you size this gap "one size too big" you grow the people around you. They will find it challenging, but exhilarating.

(Continued)

(Continued)

Use this worksheet to plan and reflect on your Multiplier Experiments.

1. Experiment Purpose

What problem are you trying to address?	What do you hope to accomplish?

2. Document Your Plan

When and where will you try this?	What might limit success?	What will you do to overcome these hurdles?

3. Establish Measures

How will you know if you've been successful?	How will you get feedback?

4. Evaluate Results

What happened?	What impact did you have on others?	What was accomplished?

5. Study Your Learning

What surprised you?	What could you do differently to improve your results?	How would you describe the return on your investment for this experiment?

6. Make Lasting Change

How will you make this part of your on-going management practice?	When and where will you use this approach again?

We'd love to hear about your successes with this Multiplier Experiment. Visit MultiplierEffectBook.com to share your story.

Finders Keepers

A third-grade student sat quietly in reflection and then said to his teacher, "Isn't everyone a genius?" That got her attention. He continued, "They might not know it yet, but they have something that is genius inside of them." Yes, it's pretty simple: We all have a native genius, something that we are already brilliant at. And when that genius is discovered, it can be extracted, polished, and made even more brilliant.

Multipliers are great explorers and miners of talent. They find it and unearth it. And when they do, they've earned some of the "mining rights" for that talent. As Woodrow Wilson said, "I not only use all the brains that I have, but all that I can borrow." When they find talent in others, they may not get to keep it permanently, but they've earned the right to borrow it and use it against the organization's biggest opportunities and challenges.

And because they deeply appreciate, utilize, and grow the intelligence of others, they offer a thrilling, exhilarating work experience that people are reluctant to give up. Around Diminishers, people "quit and stay;" Around Multipliers, they "stay and thrive."

Are you actively scouting for the latent intelligence buried in your organization? When you discover these reserves of talent, are you letting them flow to their highest level of contribution? When it comes to finding and unleashing hidden treasures of talent, we should all follow the now infamous words, "Drill, baby, drill!"

End Notes

1. Lisa Marshall, "Hitting Paydirt," *Mines: Colorado School of Mines,* July 17, 2012.

2. Names of school district and school site have been changed.

3. Name of leader has been changed.

4. Cory Booker, "Cami Anderson: Equal-opportunity educator," *Time,* April 30, 2012.

5. Carol Dweck, *Mindset: The New Psychology of Success* (New York: Random House, 2006).

6. Robert Rosenthal and Lenore Jacobson, *Pygmalion in the Classroom: Teacher Expectations and Pupils' Intellectual Development* (Austin, TX: Holt, Rinehart and Winston, 1968).

AT A GLANCE: THE TALENT FINDER

GATEKEEPERS are overly protective of their people and the status quo, treating people like resources, pigeon-holing them and limiting their visibility and growth. Gatekeepers believe:

- Intelligence is elite, relying on a small group of favorites.

TALENT FINDERS identify and label genius in the people around them, putting it to use, stretching and strengthening the talent. Talent Finders believe:

- Everyone has talent and something to contribute.
- Genius comes in many forms, and finding it unlocks discretionary effort.

Three Practices of the Talent Finder:

1. *Scout out diverse intelligence*—Gain access to the best talent, and find ways to bring this talent to their teams. People are often drawn to work for the Talent Finder.

2. *Find people's native genius*—Study people, finding each person's natural strengths and passions. **Native Genius** is something people do, not only exceptionally well, but also absolutely naturally. They do it easily (without effort) and freely (without condition).

3. *Utilize people at their fullest*—Put people where they can excel, leveraging native genius and building capacity.

Becoming a Talent Finder:

1. Utilize the genius on your team by completing the *Find the Genius Experiment*.

2. Complete the *SuperSize It Experiment* to allow a team member to grow into new responsibilities.

3

The Liberator

Between stimulus and response there is a space. In that space is our power to choose our response. In our response lies our growth and our freedom.

Viktor E. Frankl

Imagine yourself holding a crossbow knowing you have only one shot to save your son's life. Now imagine your son, holding the target over his head, hoping you're as good of a shot as everyone says.

Early in the 14th century Altdorf, a village in the Swiss confederacy, falls into subjugation to the Austrians and the tyrannical overlord Albrecht Gessler. To establish his dominance over Altdorf, Gessler raises a pole in the village square, hangs his hat on top and demands that the town folk show obeisance by bowing to his hat. Under the threat of execution, the villagers all bow. It becomes a way of life in the village until one day when a famed marksman named William Tell arrives from a neighboring town with his young son.

Tell, known for his incredible strength, skill, and rebel spirit, walks past the pole and refuses to bow. Gessler's guards arrest Tell and his son Walter, who are then sentenced to death. But Gessler, knowing of Tell's fame, devises a more cunning punishment—one that is sure to instill greater fear among the villagers and provide an interesting spectacle. The rebel is granted a single shot to hit an apple placed on the head of his son. If he succeeds, both will be released; if he fails, father and son will be immediately executed.

With the crowd looking on, William Tell and his son are brought to the village square. Walter is walked to the outer edge and given the target to hold atop his head. Tell remains on the other side. The marksman, rebel, and father takes a single bolt from his quiver, places it on the string, and draws it back against the tiller creating the tension. He then takes careful aim. Before releasing, he no doubt breaths deeply to calm himself as he faces this most cruel and difficult of challenges. Most likely his young son's breath is shallow as he attempts to steady himself and the apple perched on his head. Perhaps the son closes his eyes. Tell locks his aim and releases the bolt, which speeds across the field, splitting the apple in two.

The father and son both simultaneously experience a flood of relief; however, they actually had very different experiences in the preceding moments. While he stood taking his aim, William Tell felt pressure. His son felt stress.

What's the nature of the difference? William Tell is in control of the performance; his son is the one with apple on his head, hoping his father knows what he's doing.

We feel pressure when the stakes are high and when we must perform at our best. We feel stress when we have no control.

As a leader, do you share control with the people who work for you or do you maintain control? Do you create an environment of pressure or one of stress? The difference can have profound effects on the ability of the people around you to think and reason.

We know from current research in cognitive neuroscience what happens to our mental faculties when we are consumed with stress.

Stress is triggered by an anxiety-producing encounter, such as a principal who shuts down our ideas or criticizes our mistakes in a staff meeting. We feel exposed and vulnerable. One way our body responds is through the amygdala, the part of our brain that protects us from harm. The amygdala receives signals relayed by the thalamus from the sensory nervous system and quickly triggers the hypothalamic-pituitary-adrenal axis to significantly impact the function of the brain. This "amygdala hijacking," a delightful term popularized by Daniel Goleman,[1] spawns the "fight or flight" response that controls our decision to battle or to run from the proverbial bear. Of course, we have the same response when we encounter a "boss attack" and decide whether we should defend our ideas or back down and stay out of the wrath of our bear of an administrator. Our brain becomes driven by our amygdala, and our neocortex gets neglected.

Herein lies the problem: The neocortex, also known as our executive brain, is the center of our critical thinking—analysis, reasoning, logic, processing dilemmas, making tradeoffs and decisions. Our smart brain is starved while our primitive brain is feasting. Or in true layman's terms, when we experience stress we physiologically get stupid.

When leaders create stressful environments, they drop the effective IQ of their team. This may be done overtly, even intentionally, as domineering leaders seek to maintain power and control over their schools. However, well-meaning leaders also trigger this response when they expect people to produce outcomes that are beyond their control. Most modern organizations, including educational institutions, are the perfect setup for diminishing leadership and have a certain built-in tyranny. Any hierarchical structure makes it easy for little Tyrants to reign. And in their reign, these leaders can easily straitjacket thinking or shut down thinking entirely.

Multipliers liberate people from the too-often oppressive forces within institutional hierarchy. They liberate people to think, to speak, and to act with reason. They give people permission to think. And, in doing so, they create an intense environment rather than a tense one.

THE TYRANT VERSUS THE LIBERATOR

Multipliers create an intense environment where ideas thrive. The environment created by the Liberator is much like a greenhouse, which provides a powerful combination of protection, warmth, and water enabling plants to grow faster than if they were left on their own.

Diminishers create a tense environment that quashes people's best thinking. This environment is more like a backyard garden where a child sits holding a magnifying glass, wilting the grass, burning holes in the leaves, and zapping the bugs.

A Tense Professor

Having just received her Bachelor of Arts in speech pathology and audiology (With Great Distinction), Lois is feeling confident and ready for graduate school. Brimming with passion for her studies, she strolls across campus to the education building where she'll take her first graduate seminar in childhood language development. She's heard the professor is a real bully, but Lois is a diligent student so she figures she has nothing to fear. Lois recounts:

> I take a seat among 20 other bright and successful graduate students, all a few semesters away from our credentials and much-coveted national certifications. Confidence and anticipation seem to buzz through the room. The classroom door opens and in walks Dr. Rebecca Killen,[2] assistant professor and also the director of a prestigious university's children's clinic. You can feel a collective and inaudible gasp as she walks into the room. Everyone in the program knows that Dr. Killen is the clinic director and intern supervisor who eats interns. Perhaps, "eats" is too strong a word, but she definitely chews them up and spits them out. We all know it looks impressive to have a stint at this clinic on your resume, but only the strongest and bravest would apply for an internship under Dr. Killen.
>
> Dr. Killen is brilliant, she knows her stuff, but she teaches and leads by intimidation. I have already formulated a survival game plan: attend every class, smile, nod as appropriate, ace every test, and give her my best writing, all without making any waves or expressing any opinions. I know not to challenge her. Excellent game plan—it works well for the first third of the class.
>
> Then comes the research paper. I am actually inspired by Dr. Killen's high expectations and find security in her clear directions for the research and writing. Our finished papers need to be journal article–length and quality; I am confident mine will be. I research, I write, I am ready. That night as I drop my research paper onto the neatly stacked pile next to the rostrum, I am a competent grad student.

With the promise that the papers would be read, graded, and returned in a week, class ends.

At the next class meeting, Dr. Killen walks through the door, glares at the class, loudly drops the stack of papers she has held under her arm on the table, and proceeds to tell us that they are so horribly written that they don't warrant being read or graded. What follows is a 40-minute verbal assault on our intelligence, our competency, and our writing skills. She even says, "How dare you waste my time like this." The assault ends, the papers are returned ungraded, and then she asks, "Now who would like to go first and present their paper?" We all sit motionless: heads down, fear high, eyes staring into laps, sweat beading up on our foreheads.

It was particularly perplexing that, as a child development specialist, Dr. Killen understood brain anatomy and chemistry. Surely she knew that all this anxiety was sending our amygdalae into emotional hijack, shutting down our prefrontal lobes. Surely she knew we were all physiologically idiots in this moment!

Indeed, learning skidded to an abrupt halt that night for 20 bright, competent students, including me. Nothing was gleaned from listening to our colleagues' presentations. Instead we were knotted with fear knowing that we might be the next suspect called on to present our paper before our judge, our jury, and our executioner.

Dr. Killen dominated the space, filled it with negative judgments, and summarily shut down learning and intelligence. Like Dr. Killen, Diminishers rarely get access to people's best thinking, even when they demand it. Why? Anxiety is not fertile ground for good thinking.

Let's look at another teacher, one who understood the distinction between tense and intense.

An Intense Teacher

Patrick Kelly, eighth-grade U.S. history and social studies teacher at La Entrada Middle School, a distinguished California public school, is more talked about, more loathed, and more beloved than any other teacher at the school. Why? Liz got her first glimpse at the fall parent information night.

It was one of those nights parents with multiple children dread because, with four children, I had to get to 17 different teachers' classes, many simultaneously, defying laws of physics.

My daughter in eighth grade said to me, "Here's my class schedule. Get to as many classes as you can, but be sure to make it to Mr. Kelly's social studies class. And do not be late. And do not talk during his presentation. And do not answer your cell phone. And do not be late. Mom, did you hear me about not being late?" I left my house a few minutes early, but still found myself running the last couple blocks and cutting across the school's athletic field so I wouldn't be late. Still panting, I entered his classroom somewhat terrified but intrigued. I found a seat in a classroom with other parents who were also conspicuously on time and sans cell phones. After the standard 12-minute segment with Mr. Kelly, I left enchanted with eighth-grade social studies, ready to quit my job and go back to middle school to learn U.S. history.

Why does he affect students and parents alike in such powerful ways?

It begins with his classroom environment. He makes it clear that you are there to work hard, to think, and to learn. One student said, "In his class, he doesn't tolerate laziness. You're always working, thinking things over, and seeing your mistakes so you can learn from them." It's a professional and serious environment, which gets lighter and more fun as the students work harder. In this environment, students are encouraged to speak up and voice their opinions. Equal weight is given to asking a good question as answering one.

Mr. Kelly's expectations for the students' learning are both clear and extremely high. One student said, "He believes that with high expectations come high results. He demands our best. He makes it clear that if we put in our hardest effort, we will succeed." Another said, "He doesn't hide anything from us and lets us know what to improve on. He demands that we work to the best of our ability." No more, no less—just to the best of their ability. Mr. Kelly also gives his all. He can be spotted teaching his fourth-period class drenched in sweat after spending his prep period running the fitness circuit along with the eighth-grade students in Mr. Jones's demanding third-period gym class. He holds himself accountable to the same standard he holds his students: Give your best.

There is no homework in his class—nothing assigned, nothing arbitrary. Instead, students are given opportunities to do independent study to help them understand ideas and perform well on tests.

Students can choose to outline a chapter, answer study questions, organize ideas, or do a research project. They choose the type of work and how much of it they'll do. The students, having made the choice themselves, do the independent study with zeal. If any students believe their work was evaluated incorrectly, they can take it to the court of appeals (held regularly after school by Judge Kelly), where they learn to further articulate their thinking and advocate for themselves.

Not all students like Mr. Kelly. Some find him too tough, too demanding, and his expectations unfair compared to other teachers'. For students wanting the easy path, his class can be an uncomfortable environment. But most students are engaged by his intelligence and his dedication and thrive under his leadership. They experience his contagious passion and become passionate about civil rights, the U.S. Constitution, and their role in the political process.

Patrick Kelly is a Multiplier who liberates his students, allowing them to think and learn. He creates an environment where students can speak out but where they are required to think and perform at their finest. It won't surprise you that 95% of students in his class in 2012 scored at the "proficient" or "advanced" levels on standardized state tests, up from 82% six years before.[3]

Tense Versus Intense

Tyrants create a tense environment—one that is full of stress and anxiety. Liberators, like Patrick Kelly, create an intense environment that requires concentration, diligence, and energy. It is an environment where people are encouraged to think for themselves but also where people experience a deep obligation to do their best work.

Diminishers create a stress-filled environment because they don't give people control over their own performance. They operate as Tyrants, overexerting their will on the organization. They cause other people to shrink, retreat, and hold back. In the presence of a tyrant, people try not to stand out. Tyrants get diminished thinking from others because people offer only the safest of ideas and mediocre work. As we've witnessed with the Arab Spring and democratic movements around the world, oppressed people eventually rise in rebellion. But such uprisings can be difficult to sustain as capability for productive dissent and self-governance atrophies under such repressive forces. The citizens and new leaders must regain their ability to think and reason together.

While a Tyrant creates stress that causes people to hold back, a Liberator creates space for people to step up. While a Tyrant swings between positions that create whiplash in the organization, a Liberator builds stability that generates forward momentum.

THE LIBERATOR

The trick to the effectiveness of Mr. Kelly's class (and those of all of the other educators like him) is his ability to produce an atmosphere of both comfort and pressure. This recurring Liberator practice is based on a simple exchange: If I offer space and permission to make mistakes, you will do your best work.

Creating an environment of comfort and giving people space to make mistakes are critical parts of this equation. If our classrooms are to be true learning environments for students, they must also serve as petri dishes of learning for the staff and teachers as well.

A Hybrid Climate

The power of Liberators emanates from their ability to generate pressure without stress. They operate a lot like a hybrid car that switches over seamlessly between the electric engine for smooth cruising and the gasoline engine when they need to climb a hill or accelerate quickly. Liberators create comfortable environments where people can freely contribute, but when more power is needed, they don't hesitate to make it clear that only the best performance is acceptable.

How do Liberators create a safe, open workspace, but also demand the best thinking and work of others? It begins with the way they think.

The Mind of the Multiplier

The Liberator knows that the value he or she brings comes not from breathing down someone's neck, but rather from trusting his or her people. When pressure mounts, most leaders jump in and do it themselves. Liberators do just the opposite, giving their team space to make good choices and do hard things well. In their mind, it's like a deal: "I offer you space to think, to make mistakes, to learn. And in return for that space, you owe me your best thinking."

This is the mindset Bill Jensen had in his first year as principal at Columbus East High School. He faced an impossible challenge: The superintendent and board pressed for a senior exit exam, while his staff advocated for a measure beyond a pencil-and-paper exam. Bill agreed with his staff and was ready to roll up his sleeves alongside his teachers and guidance staff. But he quickly recognized the need to dispense his ideas in small but intense doses. When the team suggested a benchmarking trip, he said, "Get out there, find out if it's a good deal. If it is, we'll go for it." As the team traveled more than 2,000 miles, Bill stayed back—a further sign of his complete trust.

Back from their trip, the team couldn't wait to create their own plan. Bill just stood back and watched as they organized themselves late into the evening on the Friday before a school holiday. Fourteen years later, the end product—a senior project replete with career and college readiness skills and community impact—remains as the capstone experience for more than 500 students each year. When Liberators like Bill Jensen truly hold belief that their team is capable of doing hard things, they naturally give people space to experiment, but in exchange for that space, demand their best thinking and work.

THE THREE PRACTICES OF THE LIBERATOR

Driven by the belief that people can be trusted to do hard things well, we found that the Multipliers we studied consistently did the following: (1) offer choice and space for others to contribute, (2) demand people's best work, and (3) generate rapid learning cycles.

1. Offer Choice and Space for Others to Contribute

The core of Patrick Kelly's teaching approach is offering choice and self-direction to his students. The students decide how much independent study they need to be adequately prepared for examinations. They choose if and when to advocate for themselves. Patrick sets the expectations high, and the students choose whether they will meet them. But in order to create this environment for his students, he needs to be given this same environment from his leaders—self-direction and space to navigate. Patrick said, "There's no way I could have done this without the backing of my administrators. The principal and the assistant principal gave me the space I needed to teach this way, and then they backed me up."

This space was not given in ignorance but rather with full knowledge. The assistant principal, Pattie Dullea, understood the curriculum and Patrick's program in detail; she knew exactly what he was doing, and she had never forgotten what it was like to be in the classroom. She invested the time to understand his approach, and then she let Patrick teach. She also knew it was inevitable that some students would struggle and complain and that certain parents would become alarmed (especially those who wanted their children to sail smoothly through his class without challenge). When parents complained and requested parent-teacher conferences to advocate for their children, Pattie was right there. Patrick said, "Pattie sat in on many of the conferences and all that were likely to be contentious. After giving voice to the parents, Pattie would respond, 'You need to let him do this. You will thank him at the end of the year.'" Her trust and respect for Patrick allowed the parents, in return, to trust Patrick with the space he needed to teach and to give their children the space they needed to learn. Their choice would later be validated as they heard the "shout-out" from their child and many others during the eighth-grade graduation ceremony: *Mr. Kelly taught me to think.*

2. Demand People's Best Work

When leaders ask people for their best thinking and the best work, they also get their full effort.

Larry Gelwix, the head coach of Highland Rugby, stood at the center of a huddle of rugby players at the side of the field for the team's first game debrief of the season. Larry asked one question, "Did you give your *best*?" One player enthusiastically spoke up, "Well, we won, didn't we?" Not unkindly, Larry said, "That's not the question I asked." Another player jumped in, "We just dominated that team. We won 64 to 20. What more could you ask for?" Larry said, "When you came for tryouts, I said I expected your *best*. That means your best thinking out there and your best physical effort. Is that what you gave today?"

Coach Gelwix's players learned to give it all. One player recalls summoning the strength to keep playing with a painful shoulder contusion. He said, "The voice in my head was the recollection of countless practices and games when Coach Gelwix simply asked, 'Is that your best?'" He finished the game with two tries (each equivalent to a touch down).

Coach Gelwix retired recently after 35 years coaching the Highland Rugby team, with 19 national championships and a record of 410 wins to just 10 losses! But win or lose, this Multiplier coach demanded his players' best work.

As a leader, you know when someone is operating below his or her usual performance. But it takes more insight to discover whether someone is giving everything he or she has to give. But when leaders do, it offers a richly rewarding work environment that people describe as "a bit exhausting but totally exhilarating" and where people wholeheartedly give 100%.

3. Generate Rapid Learning Cycles

We all know that leadership style is contagious—probably more contagious than a lice infestation in a kindergarten classroom! If a school leader desires a stellar student learning environment, he or she needs to actively create a similar learning environment for the staff and teachers.

Are you leading your staff the same way you want your teachers to be teaching? Does the learning climate in one of your typical staff meetings reflect the kind of learning environment you want your school to provide to students? If you replicated your staff meeting's learning environment across every classroom in your school, would student learning go up or down? If you want a school where students think, challenge, take risks, learn from mistakes, and give their best thinking every day, you must foster this environment for your staff and for your teachers.

Consider one educational leader who understood the relationship between the learning environment on his team and their ability to build a great educational institution.

Admit and Share Mistakes

Mark Steed, principal of Berkhamsted School, in Hertfordshire, England, was conducting a review of the way in which the school conducted appraisals for its senior and middle management. His initial approach was to sell the idea of appraisal with his senior leadership team. This resulted in resistance and pushback as his team worried about the consequences of negative appraisals. But then Mark opened up and confided in his team, telling them about a time when he received a poor appraisal from an external assessor.

He candidly shared his dismay and frustration, but also conveyed what he had learned from the experience. Interestingly, as he opened up, so did his team. Mark's admission was a turning point in the discussion and the team's conclusion on how they should conduct appraisals in the school.

Consider another leader who talked up his own mistakes to make it safe for his team to innovate and take risks.

When Lutz Ziob took over as general manager of the education division at Microsoft in 2003, it was falling short of its goals for both revenue and reach out into the market. Lutz needed to make progress fast and could have easily created a stressful environment around him. But he also needed the organization to be creative and take risks if it was to catch up in the market. It was a classic management dilemma. If you take the obvious path, the climate will become tense and your people may become risk averse. However, if you lessen the pressure by softening the goals, then your organization becomes complacent. Lutz did neither.

He responded by creating an environment that was equal parts pressure and learning. He did this in large part by how he responded to both his mistakes and the mistakes of others.

Lutz seemed to delight in speaking of his own mistakes. When a program he started proved unsuccessful, he talked about it openly and described what he learned. One member of his management team said, "He brings an intellectual curiosity for why things didn't work out." By taking his mistakes public, Lutz made it safe for others to take risks and fail.

Insist on Learning From Mistakes

Lutz created room for other people to make mistakes. When Chris Pirie, the new head of sales for Microsoft Learning at the time, made a risky promotion that ended badly, he felt comfortable enough to go to Lutz. He admitted the misstep, diagnosed it, and tried a new approach. Chris said, "With Lutz, it's OK to fail. You just can't make the same mistake twice."

Lutz loved feedback. A direct report of his recalled a time he had to give Lutz some tough-love feedback regarding Lutz's overbearing enthusiasm for a particular project. Lutz's staff member approached him in his office and delivered the feedback: "Lutz, you are sucking the oxygen out of the room. No one else has any room to breathe. You need to back off." How do you think Lutz reacted to this tough love? His curiosity was piqued and he responded earnestly, "What does it look like? Who did it impact? How do I avoid doing it again?" After thoroughly contemplating the issue, Lutz's final comment to his employee-coach was, "I wish you would have told me sooner." And he really meant it.

Lutz achieved the climate he wanted even amid a stressful external environment by generating rapid learning cycles.

Tyrants and Liberators both expect mistakes. Tyrants stand ready to pounce on the people who make them. Liberators stand ready to learn as much as possible from the mistakes. The highest quality of thinking cannot emerge without learning. Learning can't happen without mistakes. Liberators get the best thinking from people by creating a rapid cycle of thinking, learning, and making and recovering from mistakes. They move rapidly through this cycle in order to generate the best ideas and create an agile and ambitious learning environment.

Diminishers don't understand this natural cycle and often play only in the final stage. They boldly request—if not outright demand—people's best work, but they rarely get it. They haven't created the conditions under which ideas can be seeded, cultivated, and harvested. Around them the ground is dry, cracked, and barren—hardly a good environment for growing talent.

THE DIMINISHERS' APPROACH TO THE WORK ENVIRONMENT

For Monique[4] things are new: new school year, new school, and, most of all, new position as a site principal of a suburban high school. As Monique envisions the school, she sees it as a blank slate and a stage for her leadership debut. She envisions the school on an upward trajectory receiving accolades and awards.

Dominate the Space

Monique has big aspirations, so she opens with strong opinions about directions for curriculum and policy. She wants to build consensus, so she seeks out school staff and teachers who support her views. Newer teachers rush to align with her, and a clique is formed. She seems less like a broad-minded principal and more like the diva Sharpay from *High School Musical*. She has cast herself in a starring role and has assembled her chorus line of underlings to back her up.

A typical staff meeting overflows with Monique-speak peppered with questions directed at her supporting cast, who echo back her opinion and make her look good.

Create Anxiety

With her entourage in place, favoritism and school politics take on new meaning. The experienced teachers, who have mostly chosen to stay out of the cliques, know that if they voice an opinion in her meetings, they will be shot down. Dennis, one of the veteran teachers, must have forgotten where he was when he suggested a more efficient way to monitor test booklet security. But Monique's curt reply, "Only administration sets policy regarding student testing," quickly reminded him. And if a teacher's opinion comes with any form of perceived criticism, they are sure to receive a drop-in evaluation visit from Monique the next day. People become silent and shrink. Even those in the in-group wonder if they will be next.

Judge Others

Initially, Monique's overt, hostile criticism is reserved for the dissidents and critics, but the new principal senses the growing hostility and begins to openly criticize individual teachers. Staff meetings become a forum for her venting and intimidation. When one of the first-year temporary teachers asks if she needs to check in her school laptop for the summer, she is met with, "Of course. You don't even know if you will have a position next year."

When the spotlight that Monique envisioned shining on her first year's performance dimmed, the school year ends and no one feels safe. When school resumes in the fall, voices are now silent and creativity and passion become dormant. Talent is drained from the school as, that year, four teachers find jobs elsewhere. The teachers and staff that remain hold back, give the minimum, and wait for the next leader to eventually come.

Anyone who has suffered a bout of stage fright knows that when we are consumed with anxiety, our voice rarely improves.

Instead of creating an intense environment that propels their schools forward, Diminishers operate as Tyrants, bullies, and divas and create a tense environment by dominating the space, creating anxiety, and judging others in a way that shuts down both the insights and energy of everyone around them.

When leaders play the role of Tyrant, they suppress people's thinking and capability. People restrain themselves and work cautiously, only contributing safe ideas the leader is likely to agree with. This is why Diminishers are costly to organizations. Under the influence of a Diminisher, the organization pays full price for a resource but only receives less than 50% of its value.

BECOMING A LIBERATOR

How do you begin to create an intense work environment where people feel safe to contribute their best thinking, but also pressure to perform at their very best? You might start by creating more space for others to think independently. Organizations naturally skew power to the top, and it is easy for senior leaders to find that their casual comments are taken with far more gravitas than intended. For example, a new superintendent might find that a cavalier hallway remark suddenly finds itself in a policy document.

To combat this and help your staff discern between one of your random musings and a policy statement, try clearly labeling your opinions. Divide your views into "soft opinions" and "hard opinions." Use soft opinions when you have a perspective to offer or ideas for someone else to consider. Reserve hard opinions for times when you have a clear point of view. This allows space for others to comfortably disagree and allows room for others to develop their own view.

Multiplier Experiments

Try any of the following three bite-sized experiments to become more of a Liberator.

1. **Play Fewer Chips**—Make more room for others by playing fewer chips in an important meeting. You might even pass a few of those chips around and let them multiply.

2. **Make Space for Mistakes**—Define the space for experimentation in your team's work. Let them know when it's OK to fail and when failure isn't an option.

3. **Talk Up Your Mistakes**—Give others permission to take risks by doing show-and-tell with one of your own mistakes where you lived to tell.

Multiplier Experiments

Play Fewer Chips

Play Fewer Chips
In A Meeting.

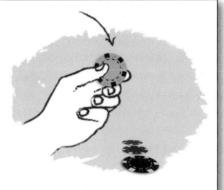

Before a meeting, give yourself a budget of "poker chips," with each chip representing a comment or contribution to the meeting. Use your chips wisely, and leave the rest of the space for others to contribute.

Multiplier Discipline: **Liberator**, remedy for "Always On" Accidental Diminisher

Multiplier Mindset:

By being small, others get a chance to be big.
By being big less often, your own ideas will be more impactful.

Multiplier Practices:

Plan how you will use your chips. When you play a chip, go big! But when you aren't playing a chip, stay small and leave room for others.

Here are some ways you might Go Big and play your chips, and when you might want to Go Small:

Go Big	Go Small
Open the meeting by framing the issue (what is the issue/decision, why is it important, how will it be discussed/decided)	When you have the urge to say, "yes, I think that too."
Ask a big question	When you want to reframe what you heard into your own idea
Offer an idea of your own (that isn't already surfacing)	When you want to say, "I did some research and the data validates that."
Redirect the conversation or get it back on track	
Summarize	
Outline next steps	

Caveat 1: You might need to allow some silence to pass after you speak. Others might be expecting you to jump back in. Be OK with silence. It creates a vacuum that draws in others.

Caveat 2: If you are worried that someone might think you are disengaged, tell them at the outset that you will be operating in listening mode and want to give air-time to others.

The Promise:

You create more room for others to contribute, and your own ideas will be more heard and influential.

Use this worksheet to plan and reflect on your Multiplier Experiments.

1. Experiment Purpose

What problem are you trying to address?	What do you hope to accomplish?

2. Document Your Plan

When and where will you try this?	What might limit success?	What will you do to overcome these hurdles?

3. Establish Measures

How will you know if you've been successful?	How will you get feedback?

4. Evaluate Results

What happened?	What impact did you have on others?	What was accomplished?

5. Study Your Learning

What surprised you?	What could you do differently to improve your results?	How would you describe the return on your investment for this experiment?
		.

6. Make Lasting Change

How will you make this part of your ongoing management practice?	When and where will you use this approach again?

We'd love to hear about your successes with this Multiplier Experiment. Visit MultiplierEffectBook.com to share your story.

Multiplier Experiments

Make Space For Mistakes

Define a space where people can experiment, take risks, and recover.

Create a safe environment where people can take risks. Clarify the area where a) your team members have room to experiment and b) where the stakes are too high to allow failure.

Multiplier Discipline: **Liberator**, remedy for "Rescuer" and "Optimist" Accidental Diminisher

Multiplier Mindset:

People learn best from the natural consequences of their actions.

Multiplier Practices:

Create a clear "water line" above which people can experiment and take risks and still recover, but below which any mistakes "or cannon balls" might cause catastrophic failure and "sink the ship." Work with your team to understand this waterline.

1. On a white board or flipchart, make two headings. ———→

2. Using post-it notes, ask each individual to list a number of scenarios where it is **OK TO FAIL** and some where it is **NOT OK TO FAIL**.

3. Have the individuals post their scenarios on the chart.

4. Allow individuals to move the Post-it notes between categories and debate which category each belongs in. Physically move the Post-it notes until the group reaches a shared understanding.

5. Push the thinking encouraging as many scenarios as possible to go into the "Okay to fail" category. Draw "the water line" between the categories.

6. Group like scenarios together.

7. Define the themes in each of the categories. For example:

    a. It's OK to fail when a) the learning is greater than the cost, b) we have time or resources to recover or c) when customers or students are not harmed, etc.

    b. It's not OK to fail when a) it violates our ethics or values, b) it does damage to our brand/reputation in the market, c) it is career ending for someone (including the leader), etc.

8. Record the key principles above and below the water line. Share this with the team.

The Promise:

Creating a clear "water line" for your team will give them confidence to experiment and take bolder action but will signal to them to be extra diligent where the stakes are high. This distinction will also signal to you when you can stand back and when you need to jump in and rescue.

Use this worksheet to plan and reflect on your Multiplier Experiments.

1. Experiment Purpose

What problem are you trying to address?	What do you hope to accomplish?

2. Document Your Plan

When and where will you try this?	What might limit success?	What will you do to overcome these hurdles?

3. Establish Measures

How will you know if you've been successful?	How will you get feedback?

4. Evaluate Results

What happened?	What impact did you have on others?	What was accomplished?

5. Study Your Learning

What surprised you?	What could you do differently to improve your results?	How would you describe the return on your investment for this experiment?

6. Make Lasting Change

How will you make this part of your ongoing management practice?	When and where will you use this approach again?

We'd love to hear about your successes with this Multiplier Experiment. Visit MultiplierEffectBook.com to share your story.

Multiplier Experiments

Talk Up Your Mistakes

Invite experimentation and learning by sharing your own mistakes.

Let people know the mistakes you have made and what you have learned from them. Make public how you have incorporated this learning into your decisions and current leadership practices.

Multiplier Discipline: **Liberator**, remedy for "Optimist" Accidental Diminisher

Multiplier Mindset:

Mistakes are part of the natural learning and achievement process.

Multiplier Practices:

1. Get personal. Reflect on your own leadership journey by charting the highs and lows of your career. Identify several of the big mistakes you've made. The bigger the better! For each mistake, identify:

   - What you did
   - What happened
   - Where you went wrong (wrong actions or wrong assumptions)
   - What you learned from it

Look for opportunities to share these stories. You might share one before someone is about to tackle a challenging assignment or at the moment they make a distressing mistake.

2. Go public. Instead of talking about your and your team's mistakes behind closed doors or just one-on-one, bring them out in the open where the person making the mistake can clear the air and where everyone can learn. Try making it part of your management ritual.

For example, you might add "screw-up of the week" onto your regular team agenda. If any member of the team, including yourself, had a blunder, this is the time to go public, have a laugh, and move on.

The Promise:

You are the most powerful role model. If they see that you've made mistakes and have recovered from them, they are more likely to take risks themselves and be willing to learn from their mistakes.

Use this worksheet to plan and reflect on your Multiplier Experiments.

1. Experiment Purpose

What problem are you trying to address?	What do you hope to accomplish?

2. Document Your Plan

When and where will you try this?	What might limit success?	What will you do to overcome these hurdles?

3. Establish Measures

How will you know if you've been successful?	How will you get feedback?

4. Evaluate Results

What happened?	What impact did you have on others?	What was accomplished?

5. Study Your Learning

What surprised you?	What could you do differently to improve your results?	How would you describe the return on your investment for this experiment?

6. Make Lasting Change

How will you make this part of your on-going management practice?	When and where will you use this approach again?

We'd love to hear about your successes with this Multiplier Experiment. Visit MultiplierEffectBook.com to share your story.

Free to Think

When people operate under stress, they shut down. With enough stress, they eventually rebel, often overthrowing their despotic leaders. To build organizations where people can think and do their best work, we need to do more than rid our organizations of Tyrants or oppressive dictators. We need leaders who serve as Liberators giving people space to think and learn while applying enough pressure to demand their best work.

Her Majesty Queen Rania Al Abdullah of Jordan, a developing yet progressive nation in the Middle East, said in a CNN interview, "In the Arab World we still focus too much on rote learning. . . . We teach children what to think rather than how to think."[5] After serving in the city of Salt, James and Shaylyn Romney Garrett, a dynamic husband-wife team who served as Peace Corps volunteers in Jordanian public schools and youth centers, could see how children taught only to memorize and repeat, a vestige of Jordan's colonial past, would never be able to envision and create new leadership and governance models. They founded Think Unlimited with a mission to educate a generation of leaders and critical thinkers and to improve education in the Arab world. They worked with the local educational leaders and began teaching creativity and critical thinking in the neighborhood schools. Next they encouraged parents to improve early intellectual development in the homes. Soon they began teaching Jordanian teachers a new model of teaching—one where teachers were more likely to ask a big question than to provide the right answer. Shaylyn described the thrill of seeing the teachers grow into their new roles, "After being a teacher for 25 years, they learn what it is like to be an educator."

Today they continue on their mission to build schools from within by equipping both students and teachers to think critically, think creatively, and use the power of their minds to create change. One teacher[6] remarked, "I learned how to improve my thinking . . . how the brain works and how I can improve my students' intelligence . . . and even my own intelligence." They foster an environment where talented, well-meaning people can be heard and where intelligence can be given, grown, and stretched through challenge.

Multipliers don't tell people what to think; they tell them what to think about. They define a challenge that invites each person's best thinking and generates collective will. Instead of rebellion, they create a movement.

End Notes

1. Daniel Goleman, *Emotional Intelligence* (New York: Bantam, 1995).
2. Name of the leader has been changed.
3. Students scoring "proficient" or "advanced" have increased from 82% to 95%. Students scoring "below basic" or "far below basic" have decreased from 9% to 2%.
4. Name of leader has been changed.
5. http://edition.cnn.com/TRANSCRIPTS/0904/22/sitroom.02.html.
6. Full remarks for this teacher and others can be found at http://www.think unlimited.org/.

AT A GLANCE: THE LIBERATOR

TYRANTS create a tense environment, one that is full of stress and anxiety and that suppresses people's thinking and capability. People restrain themselves and work cautiously. Tyrants believe:

- Creating anxiety provokes creativity and a desire to do more.

LIBERATORS create an intense environment where people are encouraged to think for themselves and feel a deep obligation to do their best work. People take risks and offer their best thinking. Liberators believe:

- People have the ability to do hard things and do things well.
- Giving people choice and self-direction instills confidence and yields people's best thinking.

Three Practices of the Liberator:

1. *Offer choice and space for others to contribute*—Invite people to choose their path, and then allow the space for them to explore it.

2. *Demand people's best work*—Hold high expectations and ask for people's best thinking, and in return benefit from the full effort of everyone.

3. *Generate rapid learning cycles*—Create a climate open to mistakes, which obliges people to learn quickly. They do this by regularly employing these techniques:

   a. *Admit and share mistakes:* Make it safe to take risk and fail by sharing your experiences.

   b. *Insist on learning from mistakes:* Stand ready to learn as much from each mistake as possible.

Becoming a Liberator:

1. Dispense your ideas in small but intense doses using the *Play Fewer Chips Experiment.*

2. Label your opinions as "hard" or "soft" so your organization can distinguish when you are offering perspective versus a definitive point of view.

3. Take the *Make Space for Mistakes* or *Talk Up Your Mistakes Experiments* to generate rapid learning cycles.

4

The Challenger

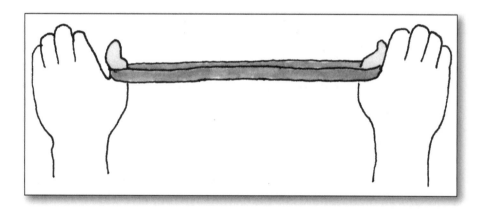

It is not the answer that enlightens, but the question.

Eugene Ionesco

Strengthened Through Stretch

Owing to its reputation for gang activity and difficult environment, Hoover Middle School, located in San Jose, California, had experienced a revolving door of principals. Knowing that yet another new principal was being assigned, the staff wondered, "What will she do to us?" They soon discovered they should have been wondering, "What will she do *with* us?"

The new principal, Amparo Barrera, a quiet woman, had a warm assuring voice, a quick smile, and a rock solid determination for the school. She believed that Hoover Middle School could morph from a school with a gang reputation to one known for academic achievement.

Year one, Amparo let her vision for the school seep into the thinking of the staff. Instead of beating and repeating her vision, Amparo asked deep probing questions such as, "What would it take for us to develop the strongest Hispanic parent involvement in the history of Hoover?" She then asked teachers and staff for their opinions. Amparo listened and scoured for validity, incorporating staff ideas into her thinking and her ideas into theirs—it was hard to tell where the good ideas originated.

Teachers found themselves drawn into the possibilities. Michelle, a science teacher, loved the mental whirl that circled around her new principal and loved being caught up in it. She said, "I looked forward to these conversations, even knowing that I would often leave her office with a new assignment on my plate." Staff meeting conversations changed from "How do we get the custodians to clean our rooms?" to "How do we get all students achieving at their capacity?"

Amparo didn't just point her staff leaders toward a high-level vision; she offered them a series of discrete challenges that they could get their arms around. Amparo called the science teachers together and tasked them with building a robotics program—from scratch!

But when Amparo had stretched the staff too hard, she quickly backed off. A teacher recalled a critical project that had her working extra time at nights and weekends. Amparo stopped by her classroom to insist that she take a day off with a substitute provided. Amparo stretched people, but she didn't break them (even if she had to break a rule to do it!).

Not only did Amparo have a knack for sparking thinking, she also had a penchant for nudging people into leadership roles. Her motives weren't clear, but the effect on her staff, the teachers, and the school was undeniable—they began to believe that they could transform the school. And they did.

By year six, Amparo had become synonymous with Hoover. As the school's transformation progressed, a new reputation for its academic achievement took the foreground. You can imagine Amparo stepping into the background to give her staff the credit when they found out that student test scores had improved and that outside intervention had been averted. Amparo knew that when you engage smart people in a shared vision and give them hard problems to solve, the impossible becomes possible. And she believed that the ensuing stretch would strengthen the entire school. Challengers strengthen others through stretch.

Now consider another leader who relied too heavily on her own expertise. She not only weakened her team, she dismissed them entirely.

Dismissed After Show-and-Tell

When Suzanne[1] transferred laterally into a suburban middle school in New England, she realized her previous first year as an administrator had some big bumps. But she tucked away her insecurities and mustered a false confidence for her new position as assistant principal. After all, with her years as a district office curriculum coordinator, she surely would know what to do.

As the first semester progressed, Suzanne was tasked with creating an intervention program for the school's underachieving students. Realizing this would require a complete revamp of the master schedule, she set out to get staff to buy in. Suzanne initially established a shared leadership structure and an Intervention Planning Committee of math and language arts teachers. But before convening the committee, she built the intervention plan in totality in her mind. The committee meeting then served as a forum to validate her ideas.

Suzanne opened meetings with agendas she had drafted sans input. She stated the desired outcome of the meeting and presented that day's portion of her preset plan. Next, she called for input. Teachers quickly learned that input offered would be met with "Well, but . . . " and then summarily shot down.

Jonathan, a seasoned math teacher, challenged Suzanne but was rebuffed with a recount of Suzanne's expertise as a district curriculum coordinator. In rapid succession, she fired technical curriculum questions at him. Pounded, he gave up. During committee meetings, the only questions that Suzanne raised were those for which she had ready, pat answers. Committee meetings were followed up with a written recap—a recap of Suzanne' ideas. If anyone else's ideas were included, it must have been in invisible ink!

The teachers soon realized that their presence on the intervention committee (which they referred to as "the faux committee") was for token input only. One bold and fed up teacher actually signed her name on the attendance sheet, *Marianne Fletcher,*[2] *here for token input only!*

Their expertise shriveled from neglect, and the committee members happily turned their efforts and their intelligence elsewhere. The staff's newfound apathy left Suzanne happily on her own to implement the school's new intervention plan, which required the creation of new classes and a new master schedule midyear. The result was a student schedule disaster that took two weeks and district office assistance to repair. Students caught in the schedule nightmare lost 2 weeks of instruction and precious learning.

Suzanne's attempt to lead were a show-and-tell for her own knowledge. Because Know-It-Alls are preoccupied with their own expertise, they tend to limit what their organization can achieve to what they themselves know how to do. Imagine what would have been possible if this new assistant principal had used her knowledge as a starting point to ask engaging questions of the staff?

In setting direction for their schools, one of these principals operated as a Challenger. The other was a Know-It-All. This chapter is about the difference between the two.

THE KNOW-IT-ALL VERSUS THE CHALLENGER

Know-It-Alls assume their job is to know the most and to tell their organization what to do. People waste cycles trying to deduce what the boss thinks and how to at least look like they are executing accordingly. In the end, Diminishers place artificial limits on what their organization can accomplish.

In setting direction for their organizations, Multipliers have a fundamentally different approach. Instead of knowing the answer, they become Challengers. They use their smarts to find the right opportunities for their organization. They push their teams beyond their own knowledge and beyond that of the organization. As a result, they create organizations that deeply understand a challenge and have the focus and energy to confront it.

The Mind of the Multiplier

At the core of the Challenger's logic is the belief that people grow through challenge and, hence, want to be stretched. Challengers lean into the tough stuff and find opportunity in obstacles. When things get tough and other managers are inclined to back off or give up, they fire up new challenges for their staff.

Challengers know the difference between giving someone *more* work and giving someone *more challenging* work. Mountains of more work (think grading papers) can spread us too thin with resultant burnout. But when we are given harder work (think renovating a curriculum or shedding a poor reputation), we stretch and grow. As a leader, do you stretch people through challenge or do you just spread them too thin?

The Multiplier understands that a good stretch can strengthen an entire organization. Let's look at one Challenger who fortified an entire organization by challenging and channeling their thinking.

THE CHALLENGER

There are great thinkers and there are great teachers; often these are different. Great thinkers are smart; great teachers make others smart. The genius of Dr. CK Prahalad was that he was both. For Liz, working with this Multiplier was one of the true privileges of her career:

> I was working as the director of Oracle University, the company's internal education function. After having spent 5 years figuring out how to train our global employees, our attention turned to developing the strategic thinking of our top executives. I went on a talent search to locate the world's top strategic educator. All signs pointed to University of Michigan and into CK's classroom.
>
> CK, a renowned professor of strategy, had a brilliant mind and an uncanny ability to see fundamental logic and unearth the assumptions that restrain organizations. He operated with precision, much like a village fisherman cleaning and fileting a fish, deftly slicing it open, removing the bones and extracting the valuable filet—all in seconds.
>
> CK's real impact stemmed from the methods he used to provoke others to challenge as well. CK was a teacher who didn't think *for* you. He made *you* think. His infectious curiosity propelled you to need to know more, to question, and to discover.

Tearing Down the House

> Our blueprint was simple. My team and I would organize a series of Leaders Forums bringing together 30 senior leaders at a time from across the company. CK would teach a course

on strategic intent. The three top executives sponsoring the forums would present their perspectives on the company's current strategy. And *voila,* out would pop leaders with strategic perspective. Or so I thought.

I should have known things would be more challenging and more interesting. You see, CK wasn't just a professor; he was a provocateur. He asked big questions that caused people to stop and think.

As CK pushed and provoked the senior leaders' thinking, it became apparent that the company's strategy was not sufficiently robust to tackle its approaching challenges and opportunities. The senior executives realized they needed to articulate a clear and compelling strategic intent that would guide the organization for the next 5 years. However, privately they confessed that crafting a strategic intent of this caliber was out of their league. So we turned to CK for help, not as a teacher, but as a leader guide.

Architecting a Challenge

Gathered around the table, we listened as he drafted a simple framework for building a new strategic intent. He laid down three distinct challenges. First, the senior executives would need to abandon their individual views (and give up their favorite presentation slides) to create a unified intent. Second, the senior executives would build the essential framework, but instead of completing it themselves, they should ask the next layer of senior managers to build out the specifics. Then came CK's final charge: I should serve as the author of the strategy. The senior executives would set the direction, but I was to facilitate the discussions, synthesizing the ideas and drafting the new framework. Suddenly, CK wasn't sounding so smart anymore. Did he know I wasn't a strategist and that he had just charged me with authoring a strategic plan for a large, multinational company?

The meeting adjourned, and CK and I sat alone in the conference room. I gave him a perplexed "Have you lost your mind?" look. CK assured me that this was both necessary and possible. You see, at the core of CK's logic was a deeply held belief that organizations grow when they are forced to stretch. Competitiveness, he taught, is borne from the gap between a company's resources and its managers' goals.[3] Obviously, he believed the same thing about people.

Because CK raised the gauntlet, we faced a collective aspiration several sizes bigger than our current abilities. Compelled by this gaping deficit, we went to work. We threw out existing documents. I asked the questions; the senior executives provided the answers. Together we architected a new strategic framework—one that wasn't fully built but had a sturdy frame.

Building the Plan, Building Belief

We excitedly, but nervously, held the next Leaders Forum. CK taught the group how to think about strategy. The three top executives jointly presented the new framework explaining that the house was architected and framed and that the group was to build on top of that work. The reaction of the room was electric. Thirty leaders could see the makings of something incredible and were honored to contribute. The senior executives outlined the remaining unanswered questions, and the 30 diverse leaders sprang into action and began building rooms, adding walls, and laying floors on the strategy.

At the end of the week, the team reported back to the senior executives, who reacted with enthusiasm and appreciation equal to what they received from the more junior leaders.

At the end of the 8-month process, 240 leaders had pooled their collective insights to establish a bold, new trajectory for the organization, with an aspiration far surpassing their current capabilities. At the foundation of this triumph was a brilliant educator and a master Challenger who asked the questions that forced the entire organization to stretch to find the answers.

When a leader stretches people's thinking, they stretch their capabilities. Are you defining the opportunities that challenge people to stretch beyond what they know how to do? Are you using your know-how or building know-how in others?

THE THREE PRACTICES OF THE CHALLENGER

Let's explore the three practices that allow Challengers to build an organization that understands a challenge and has the know-how and energy to embrace it. We found that Multipliers (1) ask provocative questions to guide discovery, (2) lay down a challenge, and (3) generate belief in what is possible.

1. Ask Provocative Questions to Guide Discovery

Multipliers ask questions that challenge fundamental assumptions in an organization and disrupt the prevailing logic. These questions are frequently the unsettling questions that cause people to think deeply, question their assumptions, and rethink what is possible inside their organization.

While Diminishers give answers, Multipliers ask the right questions—questions that provoke new thinking and focus the intelligence and energy of the organization.

Guiding Discovery

One of the best ways to seed an opportunity is to allow someone else to discover it for himself or herself. Aaron Anderson, director of strategic organizational initiatives at San Francisco State University business college, said, "When you deny someone their Eureka moment, you rob them of their opportunity to be excited and excel." When people see the need for themselves, they develop a deeper understanding of the issues, and quite often, all the leader needs to do is get out of their way and let them solve the problem.

The Bennion Center, on the University of Utah campus, was established to encourage students to engage in community service projects and activism while in college. Irene Fisher, the center's director for 14 years, was hopeful that the students would sign up for some of the city's toughest problems.

Instead of making a speech or just selling her vision of service to the poorest members of the community, Irene invited students to take a leadership position and organize other students to work with the community. She took them downtown into the inner-city community so they could see the needs firsthand. They walked the streets and observed the plight of the homeless. They visited shelters and talked with single mothers struggling to get by. Because they saw the needs for themselves, they became passionate and curious about how to create change and learned rapidly in the process. Irene noted, "University students are pretty smart. Once they see something they start asking questions. Our students asked a lot of questions and then went to work." She seeded the opportunity and allowed the students to take the challenge. Irene added, "I don't see myself as a challenger per se. I think of creating the opportunity for people to see the challenge so they can respond to it."

The Bennion Center is still thriving today, built on the assumption that you don't get the most out of people if you just tell them what to do. You get full effort if you help people discover opportunity and then challenge themselves.

Provoking Thinking

Soon after Amparo Barrera took the reigns as principal of Hoover Middle School, she and the team faced a clear challenge and threat: The school's Academic Performance Index scores had improved over last year, but the school was still deemed an underperforming school, having failed to make adequate yearly progress. They now faced possible take-over by the State of California. The administrative team, tasked with developing a school improvement plan, wasted no time in contracting with Linda Aceves of the Santa Clara County Office of Education to guide them through the process. Linda was a seasoned educator who knew exactly what the school needed to do. But she understood that the team, feeling defeated that their progress wasn't fast enough, would need to own the challenge and dig deep for the solution themselves.

Linda established a workable schedule, formed teams, and gave each a challenge. She then stepped to the sidelines (or so it seemed). Linda skillfully traveled from one team to another, peppering them with interesting questions to spice up their thinking. She asked one team, "Are instructional materials and the instructional environment geared for all students?"

She visited another team and inquired, "Has enrollment fluctuated over time in any of these groups, and if so, do the instructional programs and student services meet the needs of each subgroup?" In another round of visits, she listened to their insights and then layered on another question asking them to dig deeper. She again disappeared, while the group did the "big dig."

Linda's questions cut to the bone of the teachers' practice in the classroom, challenging past practices and encouraging them to analyze, rethink, and unearth the answers. The staff described the process as unnerving but safe. One teacher said, "We felt smart and we felt secure as we rooted through the performance data, knowing every question would bring us closer to a plan and to our own answers." The Hoover staff emerged with a plan for which they had ownership and that they could implement intelligently the next year.

Linda Aceves used her knowledge to guide the staff through a process of discovery. Instead of using her deep knowledge to give an answer, she used it to ask a question that allowed the staff to dig deeper.

Challengers ask questions that stimulate thinking and spark natural curiosity. They ask question that shift the burden of thinking away from themselves and onto their team. They ask immense questions that can't be answered with current knowledge. To find the answer, the organization must learn. Once the team is burdened to search for answers, the wise leader will offer a concrete challenge to focus the energy of the organization.

2. Lay Down a Challenge

Sean Mendy worked as a director of an afterschool program in East Palo Alto, California, a city that in 1992 had the highest per capita murder rate in the United States and a city where dropping out of high school is a norm. Sean identified with the needs of those he served as he also had faced many challenges growing up. Despite his personal roadblocks, Sean went on to attend and graduate from Cornell University, Stanford University, and the University of Southern California.

After graduation, Sean decided to spend a year at the Boys and Girls Club of the Peninsula. With a journey like Sean's, he had ample reason to tell the teens he worked with what they needed to do to succeed. But instead of telling, he challenged.

When Sean first met Tajianna Robinson (or Taji), she was a shy and hesitant 12-year-old. When she reluctantly shook his outstretched hand, he stopped her and with a big smile said, "You know there are three things you might want to do when you meet someone. First, look them in the eye. Second, give them a firm hand. Third, shake their hand up and down three full times." Taji was appalled but intrigued.

Sean continued to extend small, specific challenges to her. He asked Taji if she would take a journalism class. She did. Then he encouraged her to write a main article for the school paper, meet regularly with a writing tutor, and learn how to write a great essay. Again, she did. Next, he encouraged her to raise the bar and compete in her school's Scholar of the Year competition. She won!

Sean extended these challenges by asking the youth provocative questions and then giving them the space to think and respond. As Taji put it, "He taught me to think for myself." This allows youth like Taji to strengthen intellectual muscles and build the confidence they need to tackle the hardest challenges. Taji went on to overcome the distractions of neighborhood violence, earn a scholarship to a top-tier prep school in the surrounding area, and recently received the Youth of the Year award at the Boys and Girls Club of the Peninsula.

Whether it is CK Prahalad challenging an entire organization to rethink its direction or Amparo Barrera issuing the gangs-to-grades challenge, our research shows that Multipliers use their intelligence to make challenges concrete for others. Multipliers make challenges tangible and allow others to visualize the achievement. The confidence that comes with this is essential because the challenge will demand the entire organization to extend beyond its current reach and capability.

When a Multiplier has successfully laid down the challenge, a vacuum is created between what is required and what is known. This vacuum raises a tension that must to be reduced. Like a rubber band that is stretched to its limit, one side needs to move toward the other to reduce the tension. To reduce this tension and stretch, people begin to shift their weight and lean into the challenge. As they do, the organization creates the intellectual muscle and the collective will required to meet the challenge.

3. Generate Belief in What Is Possible

When we are faced with a stretch challenge, tension tends to force a binary decision: Do I lean into the challenge or do I let go? We base our decisions on whether we believe we will be successful. If our expectation is that we will not be successful, we let go. When this happens, the leader may feel the rubber band snapping back as his or her followers refuse to follow. But most of the time the snap is soft as staff continue to show up to the meetings, but have already mentally given up. When we believe we can be successful, we lean in and take an exploratory step. If we find sure footing, we take another until we have successfully met the challenge.

What role does the leader play in affecting this belief? How do his or her actions (and beliefs) determine whether someone takes this first step?

When Bill Green took over as principal of Valley View Elementary School, in British Columbia, he found a school resting on its former reputation, idling and going nowhere. It was easy to see that teachers felt demoralized, burned out, and on their way to becoming stagnant. It was especially obvious during lunch at the so-called burnout table where the most seasoned teachers congregated in the faculty room.

Bill had a two-pronged plan: first, to provide support and, second, to reenergize the school with the idea that the teachers were the experts and needed to be in charge. He empathized with their challenges and struggles. He brought in help where appropriate; he encouraged teachers to help each other and built "little support nests" to foster collegiality. He made structural changes to reduce teacher isolation and improve the overall functionality of the school. He looked for teachers he could leverage into site leaders. Always in the back of his mind, he embraced the concept of "start where you are and multiply." He knew the key was to build teacher capacity. He instituted appreciative inquiry to shine the spotlight on teacher successes and celebrate the magic moments.

The first collective victory came when Bill proposed an early dismissal day providing faculty with a collegial afternoon each Friday. When Bill put the decision in the teachers' hands, they raised their hands to affirm the new plan. To fuel the cycle, Bill placed a brag book in the faculty room and encouraged all staff and faculty to write down their stories and share the magic moments. The brag book spotlighted small wins, all proof that the organization was shifting out of idle.

The burnout table has been replaced with the brag book of success, and the school is in forward motion. This cycle of success was built one step, one win at a time—one person's success and then another's, each one strengthening the belief that the entire school could be successful, until the weight shifted and the challenge was met.

Challengers set a new course for an organization by provoking thinking, guiding discovery, and laying down a challenge. They then generate the belief needed for a team to shift their weight and lean into that challenge. Know-It-Alls set direction based in their expertise, leaving the rest of the organization to idle, encumbered with dead weight unable to move forward.

THE DIMINISHERS' APPROACH TO SETTING DIRECTION

Instead of using their intelligence to enable people to stretch toward a future opportunity, Diminishers give directions in a way that showcases their superior knowledge. Instead of seeding an opportunity and laying out a believable challenge, Diminishers tell and test.

Tell What They Know

Diminishers consider themselves experts on most subjects. They tend to pitch their ideas rather than engaging others to further a collective solution. Kevin, a nonprofit director who doesn't let anyone forget he has a PhD, came back from a conference blown away by a new technology solution, immediately making implementation priority one. He spouted and touted his know-how even when he had to fill in the blanks where he couldn't follow the logic. A lack of firsthand experience doesn't keep Diminishers from impersonating experts.

Test What You Know

When Diminishers do engage others, to no surprise, it is as an auditor, testing to make sure people understand what the Diminishers know or just said. When they ask questions it is usually to make a point.

On the first day of her university food science class, Ruthanne was impressed to see that the professor had memorized the names of every student. She hoped the class would be a challenging and fun experience, and this looked like a good sign. She soon learned that this knowledge would become ammo for his attack teaching style. After lecturing and intimidating the students with his amazing knowledge, the professor randomly called on students by name to zing them with gotcha questions. Ruthanne described feeling like a prisoner in his class, with diminishing hopes of survival.

Figure It out Themselves

Having squashed the motivation for anyone else to lend a brain or help arrive at a solution, Know-It-Alls are left to figure things out on their own. And unfortunately their assumption that *no one will figure things out without me* is proven true as others hold back, and the Know-It-Alls once again fix the problem and solve the puzzle.

It is tempting for knowledgeable, capable administrators to provide directives to their team. But when leaders are fixated on their own knowledge, it is easy for them to overlook the knowledge of others or to become trapped in the realm of what is already known. Can you imagine how this limits a school's or district's aspirations and achievements? Under the leadership of Know-It-Alls, intellect idles or is consumed by second-guessing what the all-knowing boss is thinking.

BECOMING A CHALLENGER

A powerful first step toward becoming a challenger is to start asking questions instead of answering them. This is a difficult transition because we learn at a young age to swiftly answer all questions presented to us. In fact, most educational leaders will tell you much of their day is spent answering questions from staff, students, and parents.

Shifting from having answers and toward asking questions is perhaps the most powerful change a leader (or teacher or parent!) can make. Liz learned this lesson several years ago while managing two big jobs—one at work and the other at home as a mother of three young children, ages 6, 4, and 2 years old.

> I was commiserating with a colleague at work about our parenting challenges. Brian also had several small children, so he listened in simpatico as I lamented that I had become a bossy mom, constantly telling my kids what to do and barking orders. I detailed a typical evening at my house: "Get ready for bed. Stop that. Leave her alone. Pick up your toys. Put on your pajamas. Brush your teeth. Go back and use toothpaste this time. Story time. Get into bed. Go back to bed. No, not in my bed, *your* bed. OK, now go to sleep. "
>
> To be clear, I wasn't looking for advice—this was purely recreational complaining. But Brian offered an interesting challenge. He said, "Liz, why don't you go home tonight and try speaking to your children only in the form of questions. No statements, no directives, no orders. Just questions." I quickly countered, "But this is impossible. I'll be home by 6:00 pm and I can't get them to go to sleep until 9:30 pm. That's three and a half hours!" Brian assured me that he understood and reiterated the challenge, "No statements. Just questions." As I drove home I became more intrigued. I decided I would take the challenge to the extreme: Everything I said would be a legitimate question.
>
> I summoned strength, opened the house door, and began the experiment. Dinner and playtime were interesting. When it got close to bedtime, I looked at my watch and asked my children, "What time is it?" One responded, "It's bedtime." I continued, "What do we do to get ready for bed?" They explained, "We get our pajamas on." "OK, who needs help?" The 2-year-old did, so I helped him while the girls got themselves dressed for bed. "What's next?" I asked. They responded with a remarkable understanding of the bedtime

routine and eagerness to act. Soon their teeth were brushed. "What story will we read tonight? And whose turn is it to pick the story? And who is going to read it?" After story time I asked, "Who is ready for bed?" Eagerly, they said their prayers and hopped into their beds. And they stayed there. And then they dozed off to sleep.

I stood in the hallway in shock and wondered, have I just witnessed a miracle? What has happened to my children? And how long have they known how to do this?

I was intrigued by this dramatic change in our home, so I continued the experiment a couple more nights. Yes, I did return to a more balanced pattern of communication, but not before the experience had a profound and permanent shift in the way I led. When I moved out of the mode of giving the answers and started asking the questions, I discovered that my kids knew how to do a lot of things that I had been doing for them. I decided to try it at work. As I began to tell less and ask more, I found that my management team was even smarter than I had previously seen. Most of the time, they didn't need me telling them what to do.

I learned that the best leaders ask questions and let other people find answers.

You can conduct the *Extreme Questions Experiment* to shift from Know-It-All into Challenger mode. Start with 100%. Try it at home or try it at school by finding a staff meeting or one-on-one meeting that you can lead solely with questions. You might be surprised at what people already know.

You might also try pausing for a longer period of time after asking a question to allow your staff to gather their thoughts and formulate better responses. A study, reported by Kenneth Tobin in the *Review of Educational Research*,[4] measured the amount of time teachers will wait after asking a question before they answer it themselves. The study found that no teacher had an average wait time over 1.8 seconds. The study also found that the dynamic of the discussion was dramatically changed if the teacher was able to hold out and wait 5 seconds for a response. Student response rate and length improved and students offered richer, more thoughtful responses. You might try asking your staff an intriguing, challenging question and then silently and slowly counting to five. Chances are that you'll get better answers.

Or maybe like Irene Fisher, you organize a field trip and take your team into the community to discover a need. Or maybe you generate belief by finding some proverbial low-hanging fruit, picking it, and creating a symbolic win that allows everyone to reach for a higher branch.

Multiplier Experiments

Try either of these two bite-sized experiments to become more of a Challenger.

1. **Extreme Questions**—Conduct this *Extreme Questions Experiment* in an important meeting. You ask the questions and let others offer the answers. Be sure to drop re-statements and comments, and only ask questions.

2. **Lay a Concrete Challenge**—Identify a major challenge and start the team by getting specific. Make it an intriguing puzzle by detailing the constraints, such as, "How do we accomplish X by Y date, with only Z resources available to us?" Then stand back and let your team solve the puzzle.

Strengthened by Stretch

Jimmy Carter said, "If you have a task to perform and are vitally interested in it, excited and challenged by it, then you will exert maximum energy. But in the excitement, the pain of fatigue dissipates, and the exuberance of what you hope to achieve overcomes weariness."

Our research, both in business and across schools worldwide, has shown that when people work for Diminishers, they give only half of their capability, but they consistently report the experience to be "exhausting." In contrast, under the leadership of Multipliers, people are able to give their all—100% even—and describe the experience as "a bit exhausting but totally exhilarating!" Isn't it interesting that giving half our capability is exhausting, but giving our all is exhilarating? We often think burnout is a result of working too hard; more often burnout occurs when people aren't given meaningful work or can't see the results of their hard work.

When leaders operate as Challengers, they get contributions from their people that far surpass what they thought they had to give, and it is this concomitant exhilaration that makes people sign up again and again. Why? Because you have offered them a deeply challenging and rewarding experience. Ask for more and you will get more. So will the people who work for you.

Multiplier Experiments

Extreme Questions

Lead a meeting or conversation by only asking questions.

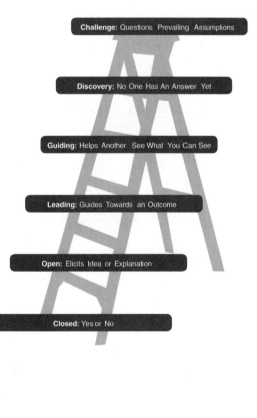

This means everything you say ends in a question mark! Or better put: Can you make sure that everything you say ends with a question mark?

Multiplier Discipline: **Challenger**, remedy for "Idea Guy" and "Rapid Responder"

Multiplier Mindset:

They want to learn from the people around them and understand.

Multiplier Practices:

1. Find out what the other person knows. Have a point of view or opinion, but bring it into the conversation by virtue of the types of questions you ask.

2. Go all the way and only ask questions! Think of it in terms of hours, not minutes.

   - Leading questions: Lead someone toward a specific outcome
   - Guiding questions: Help another see what you can see
   - Discovery questions: Create an idea or solution together
   - Challenge questions: Surface and question prevailing assumptions

Challenge: Questions Prevailing Assumptions

Discovery: No One Has An Answer Yet

Guiding: Helps Another See What You Can See

Leading: Guides Towards an Outcome

Open: Elicits Idea or Explanation

Closed: Yes or No

Caveat: If you are worried that someone might "freak out" or feel interrogated, tell them at the outset that you are taking a different role in the meeting and will be asking questions to better understand their point of view.

The Promise:

Something will shift for you. You will likely find out that people know more and are more capable than you've previously seen.

(Continued)

(Continued)

Use this worksheet to plan and reflect on your Multiplier Experiments.

1. Experiment Purpose

What problem are you trying to address?	What do you hope to accomplish?

2. Document Your Plan

When and where will you try this?	What might limit success?	What will you do to overcome these hurdles?

3. Establish Measures

How will you know if you've been successful?	How will you get feedback?

4. Evaluate Results

What happened?	What impact did you have on others?	What was accomplished?

5. Study Your Learning

What surprised you?	What could you do differently to improve your results?	How would you describe the return on your investment for this experiment?

6. Make Lasting Change

How will you make this part of your ongoing management practice?	When and where will you use this approach again?

We'd love to hear about your successes with this Multiplier Experiment. Visit MultiplierEffectBook.com to share your story.

Multiplier Experiments

Lay A Concrete Challenge

Lay down a concrete challenge for your organization.

Engage your team by giving them a "mission impossible," something hard that will challenge the entire organization. Help them see what might be possible, extend an intriguing, vivid challenge, and, then generate belief that it just might be possible.

Multiplier Discipline: **Challenger**

Multiplier Mindset:

People are capable of doing hard things.

Multiplier Practices:

1. Identify the hard thing your organization might be capable of doing.

2. Turn it into a question. Ensure your question is great by making it:

   a. Intriguing—Is it an interesting puzzle to solve?

   b. Vivid—Can someone visualize what success looks like?

3. Identify a first step that is achievable. Refine your question.

4. Ask your question to your organization. And then don't answer it. Let your team find solutions.

Caveat 1: Get the stretch level right. If it is too easy, no one will make much effort. But if it is outrageous, no one will want to try. Stretch people but do not break them.

Caveat 2: If you do pose a huge challenge, be sure to label it as "impossible" or "crazy." This allows your organization to take risks and fail and celebrate the progress.

The Promise:

When leaders offer a challenge and then create a culture of belief, the organization steps up. People contribute beyond what they thought they could. Your team will likely report the experience as "exhausting but totally exhilarating" and will want to sign up for another stretch.

(Continued)

(Continued)

Use this worksheet to plan and reflect on your Multiplier Experiments.

1. Experiment Purpose

What problem are you trying to address?	What do you hope to accomplish?

2. Document Your Plan

When and where will you try this?	What might limit success?	What will you do to overcome these hurdles?

3. Establish Measures

How will you know if you've been successful?	How will you get feedback?

4. Evaluate Results

What happened?	What impact did you have on others?	What was accomplished?

5. Study Your Learning

What surprised you?	What could you do differently to improve your results?	How would you describe the return on your investment for this experiment?

6. Make Lasting Change

How will you make this part of your ongoing management practice?	When and where will you use this approach again?

We'd love to hear about your successes with this Multiplier Experiment. Visit MultiplierEffectBook.com to share your story.

End Notes

1. Name of the leader and location of school have been changed.
2. Name has been changed.
3. Gary Hamel and CK Prahalad, "Strategy as Stretch and Leverage," *Harvard Business Review*, (March–April 1993).
4. Kenneth Tobin, "The Role of Wait Time in Higher Cognitive Level Learning," *Review of Educational Research* (January 1, 1987).

AT A GLANCE: THE CHALLENGER

KNOW-IT-ALLS assume their job is to know the most and to tell their organization what to do. As a result, they limit the organization to achieve only what they themselves know. The staff wastes energy trying to figure out what the boss thinks. Know-It-Alls believe:

- They are the expert on most subjects, and the organization is a means to putting their ideas in place.

CHALLENGERS set a new course for an organization by provoking thinking, guiding discovery, and laying down a challenge. As a result, they create organizations that deeply understand a challenge and have the focus and energy to confront it. Challengers believe:

- People grow through challenge and want to be stretched.
- There is a difference between giving someone *more* work and giving someone *more challenging* work.

Three Practices of the Challenger:

1. *Ask provocative questions to guide discovery*—Ask questions that provoke new thinking.

2. *Lay down a challenge*—Pose vivid, concrete challenges that extend the organization beyond its current reach, causing the organization to fill the void.

3. *Generate belief in what's possible*—Create belief that the challenge can be overcome, causing people to lean in and take an exploratory step.

Becoming a Challenger:

1. Conduct the *Extreme Questions Experiment* to begin thinking in terms of questions, not answers.

2. Solve a tough problem and challenge status quo with the *Lay a Concrete Challenge Experiment.*

5

The Community Builder

Debate is so much better than denial.

Julie Walters

How leaders make decisions is profoundly influenced by how they engage and leverage the resources around them. Our research has shown that Diminishers tend to make decisions solo, with a small inner circle and often behind closed doors. As a result, they not only underutilize the intelligence around them, but they also leave the organization spinning instead of executing. Multipliers make decisions by first engaging people in discussion and debate that leads to transparent decisions that their organization is ready to execute.

The Inside Track

In 2010, a Midwestern school district sets a bold aspiration: provide equal access to quality education for all students. This is no trivial ambition because one of its implications is the end of student tracking (where high-performing students are destined for the most challenging classes and low-performing students are slotted into the remedial classes).

A new image-conscious superintendent enters the district. He appears determined to win favor with influential community leaders. District demographics have been changing over the course of the last 5 years. Enrollment continues on a decline, which has forced the closure of a middle school. A large population of lower performing students from this closed school have been moved to Rogers Middle School,[1] a high-performing school. Frank,[2] the principal of Rogers, was actually eager to receive the new students, because it will put his school to the test. The Rogers administrative team takes a first step in supporting this new direction by opening up the highest level language arts classes to some of the historically lower tracked transfer students. Frank and the team share the plan with the faculty, the student body, and their parents.

As one might expect, several parents of the higher performing students complain. The new superintendent gets wind of the complaints and talks with the small group of vocal parents. Worried that these parents might spawn alarm in other community members, he responds immediately and takes the matter to the Superintendent's Council. He shuts down further conversation at the school level and suggests that a decision will be made at their next meeting. At the appointed council meeting, the superintendent dominates the conversation, presenting only his position and the position of the high-performing students' parents. The council supports the superintendent's decision to continue tracking students at Rogers and close the highest level language arts classes to everyone but the highest performing students.

The crisis was solved; parents were appeased. Several students where shifted to other language arts classes, perhaps not even noticing that they had been returned to their designated track. One principal was shot down, but the greater damage was done to the rest of the site administrators who no longer knew what the district position was on equal access. Did this mean tracking was still an option for the best and the brightest? Did this nullify the district goal of equal access to quality education for all students, or did the policy apply only when it was convenient and/or politically correct? Progress on related initiatives slowed as people became confused by the district's mixed message, wondering if they should move forward. They wondered what other decisions would get overturned. While principals and other leaders continued to attend district meetings, the real conversations happened in the hallways and in private as they secretly voiced their views and debated the merits of a tracked or open-access education system. The superintendent hardly noticed because he was too busy consulting with the elite members of the community. Substantive debates shut down when he was around.

When leaders make fast, inner-circle decisions, they simply delay the debate. Would-be supporters are confused about how to proceed and stumble, while active dissenters are forced underground and form subterranean, covert alliances to resist the leaders' actions.

Too frequently, this scene plays out in staff meetings and board meeting around the world. Too many leaders operate with an elitist view of intelligence, believing the brainpower for the organization sits with a select few. They lack the rich view of intelligence wherein multiple sources of insight wait to be more fully utilized and where intelligence is developed through engagement and challenge.

Consider another superintendent who approached the vital decision making by reaching deep into the community.

An Open Forum

Jeff Jones, a big-city director and assistant to the chief superintendent with connections to a Harvard leadership group, was assigned to lead a rural school district in British Columbia. Many wondered how he would fare in this close-knit community. Like many other areas, this district had experienced several waves of budget cutbacks with decisions made by top management behind closed doors. Previously, principals were not given opportunity for extensive input into the big-picture thinking behind the cuts.

Within his first several months as the new superintendent, Jeff discovered that another wave of cutbacks was approaching. He learned that 1.3 million Canadian dollars had to be cut from next year's district budget. Surely this was no way to win a popularity contest with either school-site leaders or parents in the community.

Knowing this was a high-stakes decision, Jeff gathered his team to design and facilitate a decision-making process. He led the effort to thoroughly frame the issue, then define both the problems and the questions that needed answers. He surveyed the options and launched a fact-finding and fact-sharing mission. He hired a new financial manager, accessed a web-based tool to give all stakeholders equal access to the decision-making process, and then outlined multiple projected cut scenarios and their effects. All relevant information was freely shared with all stakeholder groups.

The website provided much-needed data and allowed people to form initial views and critical questions. So when Jeff sparked public debate, people were ready to engage. Jeff posed questions for deeper consideration, and he encouraged questions from all stakeholders. For example, he frequently asked, "If we make this cut, will we still be able to empower our students to learn?" Although some discussions were heated at first, as people shared facts and received new information the emotions dissipated. This left the inherent risks, obstacles, and tradeoffs clearly visible and exposed. With community and district leaders fully informed, Jeff and the senior leadership team made their recommendation to the school board. As was expected, each school had to make cuts. Some were deep. But the cuts, having been intelligently considered by all, were understood and accepted. In the process of making a tough decision, Jeff built community.

When faced with a difficult set of decisions, Jeff was the Community Builder rather than the Decision Maker. He framed the issues, sparked debate, and made the decision-making process transparent. Yes, he also had a strong role in making the final decision, but not before deeply engaging the broader community. His approach wasn't an empty exercise in faux inclusion; it was an open forum for multiple perspectives and dissenting views, which generated a shared understanding and a shared commitment. The following year, when the cuts were challenged, Jeff was able to refer back to the survey tool to show how each stakeholder group had contributed to the discussions. Having given the community an opportunity to weigh in, Jeff didn't need to try to force their buy-in—he already had it.

When faced with the most crucial decisions, do you throw your weight around or do you let people weigh in? When people are allowed to intelligently weigh in, buy-in is a no-brainer.

THE DECISION MAKER VERSUS THE COMMUNITY BUILDER

Community Builders engage people in debating the issues up front. This practice leads people to make sound decisions that they understand and can effectively execute.

Decision Makers have misplaced efficiency. They make decisions efficiently within a small, inner circle, but they leave the broader organization in the dark to debate the soundness of the decision instead of executing them.

The Mind of the Multiplier

Where do you believe intelligence resides in your district? Is it at the superintendent's cabinet level, vested in a few really smart people who should become exclusive direction setters? Or does intelligence exist abundantly across your district and school community?

Multipliers hold a rich view of intelligence, seeing it in Technicolor and finding it across diverse roles and different levels of an organization. This broader view leads to the assumption that decisions should be made after bringing people together, discovering what they know, and challenging and stretching each other's thinking. Sure, this is a messy process. Any citizen of a democracy knows this. But it is in the imperfect process of pounding out issues that a community is strengthened and collective will is forged. Hubert H. Humphrey, America's vice president under Lyndon B. Johnson, captured this when he said, "Freedom is hammered out on the anvil of discussion, dissent, and debate."

The transparency with which Jeff Jones approached his district's $1.3 million budget cuts reflected these assumptions. He leveled the playing field by giving his community pertinent data, by encouraging them to carefully consider all of the ramifications, and by allowing them to express their views. Instead of closing the doors to consult with the inner circle, he opened the process and invited people in.

By assuming there are only a few people worth listening to, Diminishers rely on their own knowledge or an inner circle to make the decision. Multipliers have a gravity pull toward the full brain-power of their organization. On decisions of consequence, they lead rigorous debate that depersonalizes the issues, but builds the collective will to execute the decisions made.

THE COMMUNITY BUILDER

Lutz Ziob, the general manager of Microsoft learning who was high-lighted earlier, approaches decision making in his organization with both the mind and the practices of a Community Builder. When Lutz took over the education division at Microsoft in 2003, it was a tradi-tional education function that delivered 5-day instructor-led classes through corporate training partners. However, it was falling short of its goals.

Lutz faced a double whammy: The organization urgently needed to restore financial health, and at the same time, it needed to greatly extend its reach to ensure that as many users as possible were knowledgeable about Microsoft's technology. Lutz needed to decide if they should continue to deliver their instruction through their current community of corporate training partners or if they should pursue a bold—and potentially risky—new approach in the academic sector.

Lutz is a veteran of the technology education business, with a masterful command of both the strategy and the details of running his business. His team is diverse, precisely because he has recruited them to be.

After 15 minutes with Lutz, you can tell he is quite capable of making these decisions himself, given his vast knowledge. And given the stakes, many leaders would have felt the pull to do so. But Lutz has a bias for debate and a conviction that the more vital the decision, the more rigorous and inclusive the decision-making process should be. So he set out to engage his leadership team with the challenge at hand.

He gathered his team and framed the issue with a big question: Should they refocus their entire business on the academic market, distributing education through the schools instead of through corpo-rate training providers? Should they risk their current business model to potentially achieve significantly higher reach? He gave the team their assignments. They would meet off-site in 2 weeks, where they were expected to bring all the information they could gather and come with views about the academic market.

Not only did the team have an off-site environment, free from the daily grind, but more important, they had been given permission to think. Because everyone was prepared, Lutz could quickly frame the issue and launch right into the challenge: "As you know, the entire $300 million education business we are in has been based on a potentially outdated model. The decision we face is whether to reinforce this business model or introduce a totally new one that would push education out of the corporate classroom space and into academics where we would reach students much earlier in their careers."

He set broad parameters for the debates. He insisted, "I expect your best thinking here. Everyone should feel not only welcome to speak up, but obliged to speak up. You can expect us to be thorough. We will be challenging assumptions and asking ourselves the tough questions." Then he officially launched the first of several debates.

He sparked the debate through a series of bold questions: "Should we be in the academic space?" and "What would success require?" After each question, he let the team jump in, and he let the debate proceed.

As the discussion was beginning to reach a settling point, he pushed harder, asking people to switch sides and argue against their previously stated position. He chimed in, "Chris, switch sides with Raza. Raza, you've been for this idea, you now argue against it. Chris, you now argue for it." They would switch roles, which felt awkward for a moment or two, but soon they'd begin to pound the issues from the other vantage point. Or to broaden people's perspectives, Lutz asked his people to assume roles outside of their functional area. He persisted, "Teresa, you've been offering an international perspective on this, now look at it with a domestic hat on." And "Lee Anne, you've been looking at the technical issues. I want you to debate this from the marketing perspective." The team stepped away from their positions, and a new set of sparks erupted. Lutz loved to stir up controversy and would become noticeably disappointed if the debate wasn't charged and the sparks weren't flying.

The team listened passionately to the rich and different perspectives. They challenged one another's assumptions and often their own. They happily dropped the polite professionalism that typifies so many staff meetings and took on the challenges with an almost ferocious appetite. This was a high-stakes approach to a high-stakes decision.

Lutz did not leave debate to chance. He knew that while creating a debate is easy, creating a rigorous debate requires a deliberate approach.

THE THREE PRACTICES OF THE COMMUNITY BUILDER

Multipliers build community by engaging others in a process that is both thoughtful and energizing. Instead of making rapid decisions that spawn secret debate (often leading to a protracted implementation of the decision), Multipliers drive a thoughtful process that sanctions upfront debate. This in turn builds support for decisions that can be swiftly executed. In this considered process they consistently (1) frame the issue, (2) spark debate, and (3) drive a transparent decision.

1. Frame the Issue

Rebuilding Together is a nonprofit organization providing home revitalization for struggling homeowners in deteriorating neighborhoods in 955 U.S. cities. Every year in April, Rebuilding Together mobilizes a small army of volunteers, mostly unskilled, who descend on the homes and complete the much-needed work in one intense work day.

To make such rapid work possible, construction captains serve as project managers and size up the project in advance. With the project clearly scoped, framed, and staffed, the army of volunteers is unleashed on the project. Under the direction of the captains, the volunteers rebuild together. At the end of the exhausting but exhilarating workday, the work is done and the entire crew enjoys satisfaction from serving some of the community's most vulnerable citizens.

Imagine now the process without the careful planning and framing. Picture 50 eager, well-meaning volunteers loaded with ambition but without supplies and tools. Imagine a group hammering new wallboard onto studs that are deteriorating from termites. Or imagine a group charged to touch up the paint in a room but unable to because no one checked the existing paint color first and the new paint doesn't match.

The secret to a great decision is what the leaders do before debate starts. They prepare the organization for discussion and debate by forming the right questions and the right team. Then they frame the issues and process in a way that everyone can contribute.

Like a frame, there are four sides to a well-crafted issue:

1. The Question: What is the decision to be made? What are we choosing between?

2. The Why: Why is this an important question to answer? Why does the decision warrant collective input and debate? What happens if it is not addressed?

3. The Who: Who will be involved in making the decision? Who will give input?

4. The How: How will the final decision be made? Will it be made by majority rule? Consensus? Or will you (or someone else) make the final decision after others provide input and recommendations?

A common mistake is attempting to debate a topic rather than a question. The most productive debates are in answer to a well-defined question, one with clear, often mutually exclusive options. For example, a weak debate question is: Where should we cut expenses? A stronger debate question would be: Should we cut funding for afterschool academic support, school athletics, or dramatic arts?

Once the issue is framed, the leaders resist the temptation to jump in, when there is fire for the deed, and begin the debate. Instead, they wisely give people time to prepare and assemble their thinking, knowing the extra space will serve to strengthen the thinking and remove emotion from the discussion. They not only frame the issue, but they delineate each person's assignment. Often this assignment includes coming with a clearly thought-through point of view and evidence to support it. Interestingly enough, we find that teams come to the soundest decisions when people come in, not in a neutral position, but having established a clear opening position.

When Lutz Ziob engaged his team in the vital decision described earlier, he clearly framed the issue. He began by defining the big question: Should they refocus their entire business on the academic market, distributing education through the schools instead of through corporate training providers? He then explained why this decision was vital to their ability to expand their reach and educate as many potential users as possible. He outlined the process and gave each member of his team 2 weeks to prepare, asking them to come with a point of view and information to inform the decision.

Let's look at another master at framing issues. When Susan joined the Menlo Park City School District Language Arts Steering Committee in 2011, it wasn't just because she wanted to be sure creative teaching didn't turn into creative testing. She was curious about Allison Liner, an elementary principal in the district. She had heard good things about Allison's leadership style and wanted to witness it firsthand. She wasn't disappointed.

Allison was two things: first, a materials supplier and, next, the "dig" supervisor. Susan remembers, "Not only did she bring a warm, welcoming climate into the committee, Allison came prepared. She brought lots of materials. Her style was to supply data and information and then lead with questions." Allison viewed her position as more of a participant than as an imposer of ideas. A typical response was "Tell me more" as she led deep inquiry. When more data and information was needed, it would show up at the next meeting with Allison. Because of Allison's prep work, the committee maintained its focus, responded with their best work, and produced the required document ahead of schedule and well before the school year ended.

When a leader has framed the issues well, the rest of the team knows where to focus. But not only do they know what's inbounds, they know what is out of bounds. This framing operates much like the surgical drape used in most medical procedures.

Imagine you are sitting atop the gurney in the pre-op room while the nursing staff prepares you for knee surgery. You are poked and prepped, checked and rechecked, and handed numerous forms to sign. Then the nurse hands you a big, black Sharpie marker. You wonder how you'll sign in triplicate with this blunt instrument. The nurse then asks, "Can you please indicate for the surgeon the knee that is being operated on today?" You experience a moment of panic, wondering how there could be confusion about this. Do they really not know? The nurse asks you to write "NO" on the wrong knee and "YES" just below the right knee. Realizing you will soon be fully anesthetized, you find this comforting and happily write your final instruction to your surgeon.

Once in the operating room, another nurse places a thin, blue surgical drape over the designated knee blocking out everything in your lower half, except your right knee, which is visible through the 5-inch square opening in the middle of the drape. The surgical team sees only a knee needing a new anterior cruciate ligament. Freed from distraction and contamination, the surgical team is ready to work.

When a leader has clearly framed an issue (clarifying the question, rationale, and process) and allowed people to prepare, the team is ready for debate.

2. Spark Debate

What comes to your mind when you hear the word *debate*? Many of us have negative or cautious connotations such as conflict, argument, politics, endless discussion, opposing sides, and winners and losers. Perhaps you are like many who develop an allergic reaction to the idea of participating in a debate, let alone leading one. If you hold any of the these reservations, we invite you to consider a new association with debate: Debate is a technique for speed and for strengthening teams.

Once the issue or decision is well framed, the leader's role is a dual one: create safety for people to do their best thinking while also demanding rigor that challenges conventional thinking.

Create Safety

Lutz created a safe environment for his team at Microsoft by instituting clear parameters and expectations. By establishing an obligation to speak up, he made it safe to be vocal. His team members could argue a point of view without feeling aggressive—they were merely playing a vital and mandatory team role. By letting them know that there would be tough questions, he gave permission for others to challenge and to wobble a bit when faced with tough questions.

Here are some ways leaders can create safety in a debate:

- Ask everyone to weigh in.
- Leave organizational hierarchy and titles at the door.
- Encourage all points of view.
- Focus on the positions rather than the people representing them.
- Share the leader's views last, after hearing other people's views.

Demand Rigor

Creating safety invites people into debate; demanding rigor makes the debate worthwhile. Community Builders ask hard questions that challenge the type of assumptions that entrench organizations in ineffective thinking and unproductive practices. They dig deeper for new ideas and solutions. They search out evidence to either confirm a point of view or lead the group to embrace a dissimilar point of view. Aaron Anderson of San Francisco State University observed, "The leader's role is to listen and think through the issues and craft the single most challenging question to pose next. When you run out of challenging questions, it's time to ask for a decision."

Here are some ways leaders can demand rigor in a debate:

- Ask tough questions.
- Challenge the underlying assumptions.
- Ask for evidence.
- Ask people to switch positions and argue the other side.
- Ask people to switch perspectives and argue from a different stakeholder point of view.

Lutz Ziob uses several simple but powerful techniques to help his team move beyond conventional thinking:

The Stir: After framing the expectations and launching a series of questions, Lutz waits for thinking to bubble. When it appears that an early consensus is forming, he jumps back in to stir things up, creating new bits of unresolved controversy.

The Switch: After asking people to come prepared with a position, he asks them to drop their position and argue from the exact opposite point of view. Imagine the effect this has on a team! By arguing from the opposite or a different point of view, the individuals:

- see the issues from another person's perspective, developing deeper empathy and understanding.
- have to argue against themselves, surfacing the problems and pitfalls in their opening position.
- may find new alternatives that elicit the best ideas from the competing options.
- separate themselves from a position. When the final decision is reached, it no longer has an owner or advocate. The group owns the final position.
- learn to prepare more fully for debates. In addition to developing an opening position, they might also come prepared to argue the other side.

Brian Pepper, a principal of a newly built middle school, needed to create a team to bring the vision of a progressive middle school to fruition. He not only engaged his leadership group, but also gave a strong voice to teachers in the decision-making process. He gathered all staff and teachers en masse, but created smaller forums to encourage less vocal teachers to contribute. Assembled at round tables, he posed big questions to stimulate table talk within the smaller groups. Brian then circulated, listening to the ideas as they bubbled up. To ensure that no one voice dominated when the plenary reconvened, he invited people at random to share their ideas for all to consider.

When a leader creates a forum for dissent to surface, be explored, and then dissipate in a safe and energizing way, the team becomes strengthened and unified behind a decision. As people debate an issue thoroughly, they develop a deep understanding of the underlying problems or opportunities and the imperatives for change. They put their "thumbprint" on the decision. Because they achieved a collective understanding, they are capable of executing collectively. When we understand the rationale for a decision, we can execute swiftly.

Sure, poorly constructed debate can be time consuming. But when done right, debate is a technique for achieving speed—speed of decision and speed of execution. Too many administrators treat it like a bloodletting when it really should be conducted like surgery.

3. Drive a Transparent Decision

Transparency in debate invites stakeholders to take a seat at the discussion table either vicariously or in person. Closed doors breed mistrust and second-guessing. Hidden debate and discussion do the same. Efficient and effective debate can be achieved through transparency.

One executive we studied in the business world often held his organization's debates in a conference room they came to call "The Theater." The Theater looked like any other conference room, with a large conference table that the key players sat at during the debates. However, the room had twice as many chairs set up around the parameter of the room. These debates were open to anyone in the organization. The team called it The Theater because it was like a surgical theater in a teaching hospital. As people watched these debates, they came to a better understanding of the issues. When decisions were reached, there were people at all levels of the organization ready to execute. With this model of transparent decision making, communicating the decision and the rationale is easy because the organization is already prepared to move forward.

It would be a unique school where space was available to stage The Theater. That stated, an open theater atmosphere doesn't take a building crew to create; it simply takes an attitude adjustment. A wise leader facing a tough decision will do the following:

- Communicate the timeline and the process by which the decision will be made freely to all stakeholders.
- Hold open forums to inform, inform, and inform again, always remembering that facts and information dispel doubt. Like Jeff Jones, they will invite and openly answer all questions.
- Communicate the decision and rational. Effective leaders will be as open and transparent on the decision end of the process as they were at the beginning, again minimizing doubt and backlash.
- Give it time. It takes time to arrive at collective understanding, which in turn will lead to a collective decision. As the process rolls along, momentum builds forward motion, resulting in collective execution. But once you have momentum, the entire organization moves quickly.

How can you create transparency inside your school or district? When people can see into a process, they not only understand it, they trust it. Interdependency may create a need for community, but trust builds community.

THE DIMINISHERS' APPROACH TO DECISION MAKING

Instead of looking broadly into the community for intelligence and input, Diminishers tend to make decisions quickly either based solely on their own opinions or with input from a close inner circle. They have their antennae up for problems, reacting quickly and dominating the discussion before forcing an on-the-spot decision. Having been blindsided, people around them spin and speculate, which distracts them from carrying out the decision.

React to the Issues in Front of Them

See a bear, shoot a bear is the modus operandi of the Decision Maker. An emergent issue is irresistible bait. Clarice,[3] a vice principal in Oklahoma, was notorious for her rapid reaction time and near-sighted leadership. Having overloaded certain subject-alike teams with difficult students, she faced a deluge of vocal, angry parents.

Instead of stepping back and engaging her team to problem solve, she overreacted and made quick fixes to appease the parents. Her formula was predictable: disruptive student + vocal parent = give 'em a piece of candy and send 'em back to class.

Dominate the Discussion

When issues do get discussed or even debated, Diminishers tend to dominate the discussion, infusing it with their personal views. They are debaters, not debate makers. One superintendent put out a call for opinions on student data tracking methods. Several schools in the district had each been piloting different computerized programs. These principals had been charged with analyzing progress to date and preparing a recap of their experience. They came to the cabinet meeting loaded with input and then attempted to share it in the sliver of time they were given. What followed was a lecture about *the* program the superintendent had concluded was superior and why and when that program would be adopted. Deflated, the principals made the mental note: *Do not waste your time like that again.*

Force a Premature Decision

Diminishers tend to force decisions instead of teasing out the best option. One particular Diminishing senior leader said, in an attempt to drive closure after dominating a task force meeting, "I think we're all in agreement that we should centralize this function." A brave team member spoke up and told him, "No, Joe. We have heard your opinion, but we don't have agreement."

At first glance it might appear that Diminishers are good decision makers. They are often smart and fast. But because only a few people are included and enlightened, they leave the greater part of the organization in the dark. In opaque confusion, people turn to debating the soundness of the decision (and the leader) at the very time the leaders believe their staff is faithfully executing their clear decision.

BECOMING A COMMUNITY BUILDER

For those who have avoided debate, becoming a master debate maker can feel daunting. To get started, you might try debating like a third grader. The Junior Great Books foundation teaches a simple but powerful technique for teaching third-grade students to dig into a piece of great youth literature. It teaches three rules to adult volunteers who will lead these shared inquiry sessions:

1. The discussion leader only asks questions. This means that the leader isn't allowed to answer his or her questions or give his or her interpretation of the story's meaning. This keeps the students from relying on the leader's answers.

2. The students must supply evidence to support their theories. If a student thinks that Jack went up the beanstalk a third time to prove his invincibility, he or she is required to identify a passage (or more than one) in the text that supports this idea.

3. Everyone participates. The role of the leader is to make sure everyone gets airtime during the discussion. Often the leader needs to restrain stronger voices and proactively call on the more timid voices.

Channel your inner third grader, and try leading a simple debate using these three easy asks: (1) ask a question, (2) ask for evidence, and (3) ask everyone.

Multiplier Experiment

To drive further rigor into the conversation, you might try a fourth ask: Ask people to switch positions. Now, make the process more complete by fully framing the issue, sparking debate, and driving a transparent decision. The following experiment will guide you through the process.

Make a Debate—Identify an important decision that would best be made with rigorous thinking and collective intelligence. Frame the issue, prepare the team and lead the debate . . . not with forceful ideas, but with a sound process that encourages people to weigh in before having to buy in.

The Weight of the World

When leaders play the role of Decision Maker, they not only carry the burden of making the right decision, they also are left to carry it through to completion. With only a select few understanding the real issues, this can be a heavy burden. But when leaders engage the community in making the most vital of decisions, they distribute this

Multiplier Experiments

Make a Debate

Hold a Debate on a Key Decision.

Use debate to build the collective intelligence and will needed to execute fast and flawlessly. Identify an important decision and frame the issue to your team, ask them to prepare by coming into the debate with a) data and b) an opening position. Then spark the debate and drive a sound decision.

Multiplier Discipline: **Community Builder**, remedy for "Rapid Responder" Accidental Diminisher

Multiplier Mindset:

Bring together the people who need to be involved in the decision.
When people understand the logic, they know what to do.

Multiplier Practices:

1. Frame the issue

    • Define the question. A good debate question has clear options to choose from, such as A, B, C or Yes, No
    • Explain why it is a critical question and requires debate
    • Ask people to come prepared with:
       a) an OPENING position and
       b) information/data/evidence as support
    • Tell them how the decision will be made

2. Bring the group together and spark the debate

    • Ask the debate question
    • Ask people to support their positions with evidence
    • Ask everyone to weigh in
    • Ask people to switch positions and argue the other side

3. Make the decision: You can make it through consensus, majority vote, or you can make the final decision. Any of these work. What's important is that you lead your team through a debate process.

The Promise:

Debate is a technique for both rigor and speed. Not only does the team come to a better decision, but they've built a deep understanding of the issues which allows them to execute intelligently and quickly. When the leader gives people a legitimate chance to weigh in, they buy in.

(Continued)

(Continued)

Use this worksheet to plan and reflect on your Multiplier Experiments.

1. Experiment Purpose

What problem are you trying to address?	What do you hope to accomplish?

2. Document Your Plan

When and where will you try this?	What might limit success?	What will you do to overcome these hurdles?

3. Establish Measures

How will you know if you've been successful?	How will you get feedback?

4. Evaluate Results

What happened?	What impact did you have on others?	What was accomplished?

5. Study Your Learning

What surprised you?	What could you do differently to improve your results?	How would you describe the return on your investment for this experiment?

6. Make Lasting Change

How will you make this part of your ongoing management practice?	When and where will you use this approach again?

We'd love to hear about your successes with this Multiplier Experiment. Visit MultiplierEffectBook.com to share your story.

load. Informed by collective intelligence, better, more thoughtful decisions are made. Having thought through and fought through the issues, the community builds strength and puts their full weight behind the decisions. Through discussion, dissent, and debate they've generated collective willpower and the commitment to see this decision through, solving the intended problems with precision and potency. As Margaret Mead famously said, "Never doubt that a small group of thoughtful, committed citizens can change the world. Indeed, it's the only thing that ever has."

Too many leaders exhaust themselves trying to garner buy-in across the myriad of stakeholders in their community. Instead of building support, their work often builds resentment as people reluctantly surrender to the inevitable. Reverse this cycle by investing your energy up front. Engage the community and thereby build a strong community. Let people weigh in, and they will give you their buy-in.

End Notes

1. Name of school has been changed.
2. Name of the principal has been changed.
3. Name of the principal and location have been changed.

AT A GLANCE: THE COMMUNITY BUILDER

DECISION MAKERS make decisions efficiently within a small, inner circle, but they leave the broader organization in the dark to debate the soundness of those decisions instead of executing them. Decision Makers believe:

- Only a few opinions matter; the others are just noise.

COMMUNITY BUILDERS engage people in debating the issues up front, creating transparency across the organization. Debate drives sound decisions that the team understands and can effectively execute. Community Builders believe:

- Bringing people together to discover and stretch their thinking drives robust decisions.
- Not every decision needs to be debated, but debate is required for the critical decisions.

Three Practices of the Community Builder:

1. *Frame the issue*—Establish what is inbounds and what is out of bounds. They clearly define:
   a. The Question: What are we choosing between?
   b. The Why: Why is this an important question to answer?
   c. The Who: Who needs to give input?
   d. The How: How will the final decision be made?

2. *Spark debate*—Invite people into the debate by creating safety. Make it worthwhile by demanding rigor.

3. *Drive a transparent decision*—Communicate the decision-making process, hold open forums, and give people time to weigh in before the decision is made.

Becoming a Community Builder:

1. Lead a debate using these three easy *asks*: (1) ask a question, (2) ask for evidence, and (3) ask everyone.

2. Take the *Make a Debate Experiment.*

6

The Investor

If you want to build a ship, don't drum up the men to gather wood, divide the work and give orders. Instead teach them to yearn for the vast and endless sea.

Antoine De St. Exupery

It is after midnight at the McKinsey office in Seoul, South Korea. The lights are out, except in one conference room occupied by a project team that is 2 days away from a critical presentation to one of the firm's biggest clients in Asia. The team is led by Hyunjee, a sharp, highly regarded project leader. Joining them this night is Jae Choi, one of McKinsey's Seoul-based partners. Jae knows the team has a critical deadline and, as is typical, is meeting with the team to guide, challenge, and shape the thinking as they build the first major presentation of their findings to the client.

The project leader, Hyunjee, is at the whiteboard. She and the team are retesting the story line with some new facts that surfaced during the past week. The team is struggling to integrate the findings into the overarching message about the client's business transformation. Jae listens carefully and asks a lot of questions, as he is known to do.

It becomes clear that the team is stuck. Hyunjee sends Jae a desperate look that signals, *I could use a little help here!* Jae has stood in the project leader's shoes many times. He can see a story line that the team, who has been buried in the details, has not yet considered.

Jae offers a few thoughts for the team to discuss, standing up to take the whiteboard marker from the Hyunjee. Heading to the board, he begins to list several emerging themes, encouraging the team to view the facts from a different angle. The group is thrilled to have this fresh perspective, and excited voices are now engaged in testing, pushing, and building on the ideas despite the late hour. With the new insights coming from the renewed discussions, Jae can now visualize the new presentation flow in his mind. He feels a familiar comfort up at the whiteboard. He is tempted to lay it all out for the team so they can all go home and rest. The consultant in Jae tells him to go on and finish the job and complete the story line himself. But the leader in Jae signals restraint. He stops sketching and turns to Hyunjee, the project leader, checking to see if she is comfortable with the new direction. Seeing the smile on her face, Jae says, "Okay . . . looks like we've got a new line of thinking to run with. Let's see what you can do with this." He then hands the pen back to Hyunjee, who resumes command of the process and leads the team to build an outstanding presentation for the client.

Surely it was tempting for Jae to jump in, rescue the struggling team, and drive the presentation to completion himself. He would have felt like a hero. And it was appealing for the team to let him do it, given the late hour. But Jae's proclivity to invest in people and their development won out. Jae reflected on the leader's role: "You can jump in and teach and coach, but then you have to give the pen back. When you give that pen back, your people know they are still in charge."

When something is off the rails, do you take over or do you invest? When you take the pen to add your ideas, do you give it back? Or does it stay in your pocket? When leaders fail to return ownership, they create dependent organizations. Diminishers jump in, save the day, and drive results through their personal involvement.

Multipliers invest in the success of others. They may jump in to teach and share their ideas, but they always return accountability. When leaders return the pen, they cement the accountability for action where it should be. This creates organizations that are free from the nagging need of the leader's rescue.

Multipliers enable others to operate independently by giving other people ownership for results and investing in their success. Multipliers can't always be present to perform emergency rescues, so they ensure people on their teams are self-sufficient and can operate without their direct presence.

We know that the best educators prepare their students to perform well not just in their classroom but also long after the students leave it. The best leaders do the same. They ask the question: How do I lead so my team can act intelligently and deliver results with or without my direct involvement? In this chapter, we'll look at how Multipliers drive immediate performance while also building a legacy—an organization that can act intelligently and deliver results without their direct involvement.

THE MICROMANAGER VERSUS THE INVESTOR

When administrators drive results through their personal involvement, perhaps it is driven by a desire to be the hero and rescue the day. But it might be based in a subtle but powerful belief that their staff just won't be able to figure it out without their involvement. Either way, they jump in, give commands, and get results. But they don't lead. They don't even manage. They micromanage—the lowest form of administrative skills. When administrators micromanage, they may get the job done, but they often get inferior results and they create a leader-dependent organization.

Ruining the Race

Principal Georgia Rudman[1] marched into her first year at an urban Western elementary school with a purpose. She was the kind of administrator who knew exactly what she wanted and how to get it. She was notorious for poking her head in and out of classrooms (as if to catch teachers in a mistake), and the click-clack of her shoes was an early storm warning that sent shivers down teachers' spines.

The social committee, charged with maintaining a sense of community across the school through celebration, was surprised to find their new principal handing them responsibility for planning the annual Field Day, the most treasured school event. However, they learned very quickly that Georgia didn't ever really let go.

Regardless, the team had an appetite for success, taking complete ownership to deliver a day all students would remember fondly. The team masterminded a schedule that would make most air traffic controllers envious, each class's movement from activity to activity clearly charted like a flight plan. The day, including a rainy-day back up Plan B, was carefully designed, impervious to disaster, and carefully outlined in detail in a project review sheet that Georgia required and reviewed regularly.

The field day finally arrived and with it came torrential rains, literally and figuratively. The team was disappointed but was fully ready to implement Plan B, at least until Georgia jumped in. She quickly vetoed the plan and rejiggered the schedule to deliver an indoor field day. No time for discussion, just do it. The team's ownership washed away as Georgia took over. They were now left to deal with the bloody reality of burlap sack races in the concrete hallways, especially with only one nurse on staff. Several skinned knees, and many complaints later, the day finally ended. The injuries healed, but the team was permanently damaged.

Saving the day actually ruined the day. Not only this one, but many others as Georgia's team learned to hold back and give her the control she would inevitably take. This leader jumped in, becoming a wet blanket that extinguished the energy and creativity of her team.

In contrast, let's look at another leader, whose presence fanned the flames of her team's ambition and capability.

Crossing the Finish Line

In its seventh year of operation, KIPP Indy, a public college preparatory middle school dedicated to preparing students in the underserved communities of Indianapolis for success in college and life, faced difficult news: Its charter was in jeopardy and the principal was leaving after only one year. Part of the problem was that KIPP Indy had wandered from its core KIPP path. The KIPP approach, designed to produce graduates who own their journey "to and through" college, starts with detailed, nonnegotiable rules covering arrival, dismissal, and everything in between. These aren't rules for the sake of having rules; these rules hold every KIPP family member accountable. KIPP Indy had moved away from these tenets and the results showed—high teacher turnover, disappointing test scores, and risk of loss of charter reauthorization.

Emily Pelino, who was finishing her first year as assistant principal, was faced with a decision presented by the board: Help us select your new boss or take the job yourself. Emily hesitated, but took the position because she saw enormous potential for the school.

The first step would need to be a return to the basics of the KIPP philosophy. The KIPP pillars, such as High Expectations and Choice & Commitment, naturally lend themselves to a transfer of ownership to all those involved. It would have been tempting for Emily to simply remind everyone of the rules and nag them into submission. Instead of doing this, she gave accountability to the staff.

Emily, along with her leadership team, decided to overhaul the more than 30 procedures. With the teacher leaders in the room, Emily, who was now the principal, said, "We (the leadership team) don't have the answers and we don't see the problems you see. This is going to take all of our brains to figure out." Honoring the smarts within the building and beyond, Emily handed over the binder of KIPP Network best practices to the teacher leaders, giving them responsibility to redefine the procedures that would return accountability to the students and save the charter. The end result was the "Details Matter" manifesto not only detailing the routine teacher and student procedure, but, most important, explaining why it mattered to every KIPP family member in the school.

When it came time to improve teacher observation, Emily and the leadership team put the teachers in charge, clearly "handing them the pen." Instead of administrators popping into teachers' classrooms to watch and critique, teachers were invited to openly ask for and offer observation to peers. The administrative team still played their role by formally evaluating, but they understood that the teachers were likely to have a different, if not better perspective. Teachers were given freedom and flexibility once the team created specific focus areas for observation based on trends and goals within the school. One teacher at KIPP Indy said, "I've been observed more times in the last week than I was in the last 3 years at my old school." And the best part was this teacher asked for it, and acted on it.

Over the next 2 years, the halls and classrooms developed a new energy and commitment to mission. The difference is apparent, not just in improved test scores (a steady 30% pass rate climb over the past 4 years), but in overall engagement. Now, 78% of KIPP teachers feel that KIPP Indy is a good place to work. One teacher said, "When I first started I was inspired by the idea of KIPP, but when I saw it implemented in a rigid, militaristic way I lost the inspiration." She has witnessed a shift in ownership that has renewed her energy.

Instead of resuscitating the faltering rulebook, Emily was able to transform the school through the energy of her teachers. Her challenge was not to rescue a troubled program but to let them run the path to success.

As a leader, it can be difficult to sit on the sidelines to watch your team run the plays. Georgia started strong by giving ownership to the planning team, but she struggled to stay on the sidelines when they encountered an obstacle. In contrast, Emily gave ownership to the teacher leaders and coached her team from the sidelines. As a leader, how do you keep yourself on the sidelines when you think you can push the team to a victory? What procedures, processes, and rewards in our schools might drive a leader to jump back in? How might the learning opportunity outweigh the perceived consequences of not taking over?

During the 1908 Olympic Marathon, Dorando Pietri, the Italian favorite, entered the stadium laps ahead of the nearest runner. However, during the last 500 meters he began to falter, stumbling, nearly unconscious. In a moment of compassion, the officials stepped in to help Pietri, lifting him to his feet and supporting him gently by the elbow as he tottered across the finish line, placing first.[2] Afterward he was disqualified and the medal revoked due to the help. What would have happened had he been allowed to cross the finish line without assistance—would he have won? What would have happened if the officials had allowed him to struggle on his own? We will never know. The challenge to leaders is to offer support and challenge without ruining the race.

THE INVESTOR

In their role as Investors, Multipliers define ownership upfront and let others know what is within their charge and what they are expected to accomplish. They then invest in the genius of others and teach and coach and nurture that genius. They back people up, infusing the resources they need to be successful and to be independent.

When they invest, they expect a return. They give others ownership, but in exchange for this ownership, they hold people accountable. They preserve accountability and stewardship, not to be ruthless, but to complete a cycle that creates extraordinary growth of intelligence and capability in others.

The Mind of the Multiplier

Multipliers shift the burden of accountability onto others because they hold a powerful belief: *People perform at their best when they have natural responsibility and know someone is counting on them.* Accountability raises the stakes, sharpens our focus, and creates a positive pressure to perform. When leaders distribute accountability, they not only deliver results, they build other leaders—leaders at all levels.

In 2010, Los Altos School District, which serves 4,500 students, formulated a bold new vision: Revolutionize learning for all their students by 2015. Alyssa Gallagher, assistant superintendent of curriculum and instruction, was to lead the charge. Alyssa, a former principal, was passionate about improving the student experience. This was a natural role for her, and given the high visibility, it would have been easy for her to drive the initiative herself. But Alyssa knew that top-down initiatives rarely work and could see that there were talented people who were underutilized. Instead of seeing the teachers as the resistance, she saw them as leaders in the movement. And rather than asking, "How do I get this done?" Alyssa asked, "How do we empower and excite our teachers to lead this revolution?"

After the successful Khan Academy pilot, mentioned in Chapter 2, she gave the four carefully selected teachers further ownership, inviting them to serve as coaches, helping the next 50 teachers integrate blended learning strategies into their classrooms. Teachers were experiencing success and momentum was building, but there was a need for greater training on truly integrating technology into the overall instructional program.

Capitalizing on the momentum and energy, Alyssa made an attractive offer to other teachers: We'll invest in you to grow your ideas. You'll have access to these coaches and additional technology tools and receive extra professional development, but we'll expect you to be lead learners and teach others at your site.

Instead of having to be dragged into the new summer professional development program, teachers were thrilled. So many teachers applied that there had to be a selection process to choose the 24. The 24 lead learners were not given a specific list of what to do but

were asked to think about ways to share knowledge, support colleagues in transforming instruction, and ultimately make an impact.
Creative solutions such as a "Genius Bar" every morning in the staff
room and "Appy Hour" once a month to discuss new applications in
the classroom started to be implemented by lead learners at every site.

Alyssa had the mind of a Multiplier. She saw that people grow
and perform best when they know others are counting on them. Not
only did the district start revolutionizing learning, it began building
leaders at all levels.

THE THREE PRACTICES OF THE INVESTOR

Investors produce organizations that go beyond them—beyond their
physical presence, beyond their abilities, and beyond their biggest
aspirations. Here is what they do: (1) give others ownership, (2) provide backup, and (3) hold people accountable.

1. Give Others Ownership

Larry Gelwix stood on the side of the rugby pitch watching his
high school team practice. He thought back to the first team he had
coached to the National Championship. He remembered their pre-
dawn training sessions.

The team in front of him was good, to be sure. They were learning
the game, but he noticed they didn't have the physical stamina of
previous teams. Larry felt stuck. It wasn't like he hadn't tried. He
reminded them at practice all the time. They would nod their heads,
but then they didn't do it.

He could cancel practices and hold fitness training in its place, but
that risked the skill level of the team. He could yell at them, but that
would only work for a day or two. Larry leaned over to an associate
coach and said, "We need to turn this over to the captains!"

The next day, Larry stood up, walked quickly to the chalkboard,
and drew a line from one side of the board to the other. He said,
"We have 6 weeks left until the finals, and it takes a pretty good athlete
6 or 7 weeks to build the endurance he needs." The coaches and captains were listening to every word. He continued, "If we figure this out
now, we can win Nationals. If we can't, we'll be running on empty."

Larry said, "There are two options: The coaches can keep trying
to figure something out, or you as the captains can take ownership for
finding a solution. What should we do?"

There was a pause. Then the captain of the backs said, "We'll take it on." Larry said, "Right now I own this challenge. Once you take it on, you'll own it completely. We'll expect an update from you 2 weeks from today, but we won't bug the team at all."

After answering a few questions, Larry and the other coaches were excused. The solution the four captains devised was to divide the team into small groups of four to six people, each with its own leader. The captains would keep the subgroup leaders accountable, and the leaders would keep the players accountable. The smaller groups met before or after school for fitness training for weeks, and the team soon became one of the fittest in the 35 years Larry had been coaching. They went undefeated all season and won the National Championship.

When the Investor names the lead, ownership shifts from the leader to the new owner, much like the transfer of title on a house. However, in the name of collaboration, many organizations opt to share responsibility, obfuscating the distinction between leader and contributor and creating fuzzy ownership. These collaborative efforts are often doomed to fail either because (a) no leaders emerge as people aren't clear what they are in control of or don't want to step on any toes or (b) too many leaders emerge, some operating with sharp elbows, and there is chaos. Either way, the result is the same: great intentions, but little progress. Multipliers put other people in charge of a clearly defined challenge and with a well-scoped responsibility. When they do, a burden shifts. The new owner(s) now holds the burden of thinking and moving the work forward. And with this burden comes the accountability for and blessings of its success.

2. Provide Backup

When Investors establish an ownership position, they don't just leave the person to suffer alone or wait until he or she fails and then come to the rescue; they begin investing. They protect their investment by making sure the person has access to the resources needed to deliver on his or her accountability. They keep the ownership with the other person, but they back the person up by teaching, coaching, infusing means, and, at times, running interference.

Tom Demeo is the astute principal of the Carihi Secondary School, in Campbell River, British Columbia. His school, like the nearby competing high school, faced a government mandate to develop and implement a graduation portfolio assessment tool. The mandate was sweeping across his province, but enthusiasm for implementing this assessment was not sweeping across his school community.

Tracy Kennedy, Carihi's career counselor, and Kim, her counterpart at Timberline Secondary School, were among those who had never done anything like this before and had no idea where to begin. Tom viewed Tracy's potential differently. He had been analyzing her abilities and felt she was the right person to lead this charge. Tom sat down with Tracy and asked her to lead the multi-year initiative. He told her she would be fully in charge and affirmed his belief that she would do a great job. They agreed on the endgame plan to design and implement a portfolio assessment that would satisfy the government mandate, meet the needs of both high schools, and be supported by the community. Had you been in the meeting, you would have seen the ownership transfer from Tom to Tracy as she accepted the challenge and felt a growing pressure.

Tom then backed away and assisted from the sidelines. He checked in regularly and operated as a sounding board. When Tracy encountered problems, Tom was careful not to rescue her. He instead scrounged up the resources that she and the team needed to resolve the problem. Tracy moved forward feeling a near-perfect balance of pressure and support. She reflected, "I knew I was working in a safety zone. I could go to Tom at any time and he would back me up." In this dual state, Tracy operated with confidence, giving the project her all.

Both high schools successfully implemented the new assessment program, and a newfound collegiality was built between these rival schools. Sure, there was still a fierce competition on the basketball court, but when it came to introducing a portfolio graduation assessment, the staff was on the same team. The project was a success: It was fully integrated into the school's counseling program and accepted by the school community.

Tom's approach could be described in short: *Back 'em up, turn 'em loose.* On some of your vital projects, have you handed over ownership and turned your team loose? If so, how are you backing up your team? Having transferred ownership, the Investor plays backup.

3. Hold People Accountable

The best leaders not only know how to transfer ownership to others, they know how to keep it there. This is no simple task because, like a helium balloon in a room, accountability tends to float upward. When staff experience problems, they naturally bring them to the attention of senior leaders. Unless those leaders have a way of holding a problem in place or returning it to its rightful owner, it drifts back to them.

Multipliers treat accountability as a trusted obligation: given out clearly, taken for oneself rarely, and taken back only in the most dire of circumstances. Let's look at a leader who not only gave away ownership but, when faced with its attempted return, he gave it back. Liz recounts learning this lesson while working for Kerry Patterson during her dream internship.

Kerry Patterson, a former professor of organizational behavior at the business school that I attended, was known for his brilliant but slightly demented mind. Kerry is what happens when you pack an Einstein-size brain into a Danny DeVito–size body. Everyone in my graduate program wanted to work as a summer intern for Kerry, but I managed to get the job through some combination of faculty recommendation and advanced Jedi mind tricks.

As in most internships, I did an assortment of odd jobs, and my favorite was editing anything that Kerry wrote. On this particular day, I was editing a program overview that Kerry had written. I did the usual edit. I found and fixed typos and grammar errors. I rewrote a few sentences that were awkward. I then stumbled onto a particularly troublesome tangle of words. I tried unsuccessfully to rewrite the sentences. It was too big of a mess for me to fix. I figured Kerry, with his great big brain, would know best how to fix it, so I labeled it as awkward by noting the standard editorial term, "AWK," in the margin. I completed my work and returned the document to Kerry's desk.

About an hour later, Kerry returned from a meeting to find my edits on his desk. I suspected he had read them because I could hear him marching down the hall toward my office. His pace indicated that he wasn't coming to say thank you. He burst across the threshold and marched straight to my desk. Without so much as a "hello," he dropped the document in front of me with a dramatic thump, looked me straight in the eye, and said, "Don't ever give me an A-W-K without an F-I-X!" With a twinkle in his eye, the consummate teacher turned and left.

Point taken. I worked a little harder, applied a little more brainpower, and I fixed the awkward sentences. I snuck back into Kerry's office and returned the now-complete edit to his desk. Kerry continued to teach and to write prolifically, and he is the author of four best-selling books. I learned from Kerry one of the most important professional lessons: Never give someone an A-W-K without an F-I-X. Don't just identify the problem; find a solution.

When we ask for the F-I-X, we give people an opportunity to complete their thinking and their work. We encourage them to stretch and exercise intellectual muscles that might otherwise atrophy in the presence of other smart, capable people. Multipliers never do anything for their people that their people can do for themselves.

What problems (or A-W-Ks) do you need to return to their rightful owners? Are you allowing people to complete their own work, or do you rescue? If you are jumping in to help too early or too often, your team might be feeling the diminishing effects of the Micromanager.

THE DIMINISHERS' APPROACH TO EXECUTION

What causes leaders to micromanage? Driven by a belief that *no one will figure it out without me*, they hold onto the ownership for important work. Or when they do temporarily let go, they jump in and snatch it back at the first sign that someone isn't figuring it out.

Maintain Ownership

The approach of the Micromanager is captured in a comment made by a staff member of a prominent professor: "I can't make any decisions. I don't have lead in my pencil until Dr. Yang[3] says that I do." Diminishers don't trust others to figure it out for themselves, so they maintain ownership and those they supervise are never able to contribute at their fullest.

Jump In and Out

Micromanagers hand over work to others, but they take it back when problems arise. They get lured in like a fish to the shiny objects on a fisherman's line. Emergent problems and big hurdles are irresistible bait for Diminishers. They are hooked on the feeling of importance as people become dependent on them and their brilliance to deliver results. The problem is that they don't just get pulled in and stay put; they spring in when an issue appears on their radar and, when the fun is over, spring back. They are "bungee bosses," creating dependency, disengagement, and disruptive chaos.

Snatch It Back

When you're on the ground in the middle of a crisis, it's hard enough to quickly resolve the problem. Now consider attempting to intervene via cell phone, 100 miles away. Well, that's just what Cecil,[4] the districtwide curriculum leader, did when he got word from an attendee (and a longtime friend) that the team he had asked to plan and run a professional development program was behind schedule. They had technical difficulties, and the speaker was a no-show. The team now considered several options to recover and began to take action. But their progress was interrupted when each of them began fielding Cecil's phone calls, three to four per person. Cecil was instructing from afar, describing exactly how they should recover the day. Unfortunately he couldn't see the dull murmur growing into an angry roar as the hot and sweaty participants sat in the sweltering gym. His attempts to snatch it back and dictate from afar were further delaying the event and preventing a solution.

Too many administrators haven't learned the first lesson of management: The job of the manager is to flow work to his or her team and then *keep it there*. When managers take work back, not only do they end up doing all the work (which they inevitably come to resent), they deny their team of the natural learning and accountability needed for personal growth.

And because Micromanagers don't use the full complement of talent, intelligence, and resourcefulness available to them, capacity sits idle in their organizations. To counter this, they continue to ask (or just wistfully yearn) for more resources, wondering why people aren't more productive and are always letting them down.

BECOMING AN INVESTOR

Investors not only engage people through delegating responsibilities, they extend assignments that stretch thinking and capability. They grow the people around them, which grows their school's ability to tackle the next major challenge. They create a virtuous cycle of success.

But the best leaders understand that cycles of success are fueled by cycles of failure. Success is born when someone is given responsibility, allowed to make reasonable choices (some of which inevitably will lead to mistakes and failure), and learn from correcting his or her mistakes. To nurture success, leaders must nurture failure as well.

Let Nature Take Its Course

Nature is the most powerful teacher. We can easily forget when consequences are artificially imposed on us. But we remember and learn deeply when we experience the natural consequences of our actions. A Wiseman family vacation to Maui, Hawaii, served a good teacher:

> We parked ourselves on the beach at the very end of Ka'ana pali at the base of Black Rock point. It is a beautiful beach, but because the ocean confronts the huge black rock jutting out of the beach there, the surf can be rough. My 3-year-old son Christian was fascinated by the ocean and kept straying out of the baby waves and into the dangerous surf. The scene is familiar to every parent. He would venture out too far, then I would go fetch him back, get down at eye level, and tell him about the power of the ocean and why it was too dangerous for him to be out this far. He would resume playing, forget my teaching, and venture out again. We repeated this futile cycle several times.
>
> I decided it was time for him to learn the lesson from Mother Nature instead of from Mom. I watched for a midsize wave to come toward shore. I selected one that would give him a good topple but wouldn't sweep him off to Japan. Instead of pulling him back in as the wave approached, I let him venture out. And rather than grabbing his arm and lifting him out of the water, I simply stood by his side. Several nearby parents looked alarmed as they saw the wave coming. One tried to get my attention by giving me that "bad mother" look. I assured him I was on duty but as more of a teacher than a lifeguard. The wave came in and instantly dragged Christian under the surf and tossed him around several times. After a good tumble, I pulled my 3-year-old back up to safety. After he caught his breath and spit out the sand, we had a talk about the power of the ocean. This time he seemed to understand and now stayed closer to shore.

Nature teaches best. When we let nature take its course and allow people to experience the natural consequences of their actions, they learn most rapidly and most profoundly. When we protect people from experiencing the natural ramifications of their actions, we stunt their learning and development.

Letting nature teach doesn't mean letting a major project fail. Find the "smaller waves" that will provide natural teaching moments, without catastrophic outcomes.

There are natural consequences to our mistakes, but there are also natural consequences to good decisions. Allow people to experience the full force of their successes. Step out of the way, give them credit, and let them reap the full benefits of their victories.

Multiplier Experiments

You can try the following bite-sized experiments to become more of an Investor.

1. **Give 51% of the Vote**—When John Chambers, CEO of Cisco, was hiring his first vice president into his growing company, he said, "Doug, when it comes to how we run this area of the company, you get 51% of the vote (and you're 100% responsible for the result). Keep me in the loop and consult with me as you go." If your boss gave you 51% of the vote, how would you operate? You probably wouldn't waste time second-guessing yourself and your standing. But you would probably also consult with your boss on important decisions. Let someone know he or she is in charge by giving him or her the majority vote. Give 51%, and keep just 49% for yourself. Watch what happens.

2. **Give It Back**—It was the end of a wonderful double family vacation, the kind where the adults sit on the couch and visit while the kids run wild with their cousins. As the vacation drew to a close, Fronda turned to her sister-in-law and said, "I've learned so much about parenting by watching you." Her sister-in-law was perplexed because she couldn't remember any moments of brilliant parenting. Fronda continued, "You never solve your children's problems for them. When my children come to me with a problem, it's so easy to jump up and fix it. You always hand it back to them. You say essentially the same thing each time: 'How do you want to solve that?' or 'What do you think we should do?' They seem to find an answer and continue on their way." When your staff brings you a problem, remind yourself that it's likely they already have an answer in mind. Ask them how they think it can be solved. If they are truly stuck, offer a modicum of help, but remember to give the pen back.

Multiplier Experiments

Give 51% of the Vote

Put someone else in charge by giving that person the majority vote.

Instead of delegating work, let people know that they (not you) are in charge and accountable. Tell them they get 51% of the vote, but 100% of the accountability.

Multiplier Discipline: **Liberator** and **Investor**, remedy for "Always On" and "The Rescuer" Accidental Diminisher

---

Multiplier Mindset:

People operate at their best when they are in charge and held accountable for their work.

Multiplier Practices:

1. Identify the project you are going to transfer to a team member

2. Describe the project and answer questions to ensure their understanding

3. Give them the majority vote and give it a number to make it concrete

For example, tell them they have 51% of the vote and you have only 49%. Or go wild and make it 75/25%. Anything over 50% will carry the message: You are in charge. You get final decision.

Be sure they understand what 51% (or more) means:

- You are in charge (hence, I am not)
- You get to make the final decisions (I will weigh in, but if we disagree, you make the call)
- I expect you to be the one to move things forward (I will participate, but will follow your lead)

You can really punctuate the point by saying (with a twinkle in your eye!)

"You're 51%. I'm 49%. So, I'm taking this off my to-do list."
Implication: "I'll assume it is on yours!"

Caveat: Don't give someone 51% (or more) of the ownership unless you really mean it. Pulling it back will put an end to their willingness to take the lead.

The Promise:

When you give someone 51% of the vote, they will lead and operate with confidence. Retaining 49% of the vote encourages them to consult and collaborate with you, but with them in the lead position.

Use this worksheet to plan and reflect on your Multiplier Experiments.

1. Experiment Purpose

What problem are you trying to address?	What do you hope to accomplish?

2. Document Your Plan

When and where will you try this?	What might limit success?	What will you do to overcome these hurdles?

3. Establish Measures

How will you know if you've been successful?	How will you get feedback?

4. Evaluate Results

What happened?	What impact did you have on others?	What was accomplished?

5. Study Your Learning

What surprised you?	What could you do differently to improve your results?	How would you describe the return on your investment for this experiment?

6. Make Lasting Change

How will you make this part of your ongoing management practice?	When and where will you use this approach again?

We'd love to hear about your successes with this Multiplier Experiment. Visit MultiplierEffectBook.com to share your story.

Multiplier Experiments

Give It Back

Give ownership back to the person it belongs to.

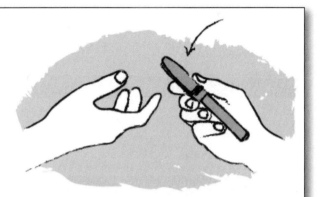

When someone brings you a problem that you think they are capable of solving, give it back to them and ask for the "F-I-X."* Play the role of coach rather than problem solver.

If someone legitimately needs help, jump in (take "the pen"*) and contribute, but then clearly give ownership ("the pen") back.

Multiplier Discipline: **The Investor**, remedy for "Rescuer" Accidental Diminisher

---

Multiplier Mindset:

People are smart and will figure it out.

Multiplier Practices:

1. **Ask for the F-I-X:** When someone brings you a problem, ask them to complete the thought process and provide a solution (an F-I-X)*. Use coaching questions like these to offer help, but maintain their ownership for the work:

   - What solution(s) do you see to this problem?
   - How would you propose we solve this?
   - What would you like to do to fix this?

2. **Give the "pen" back:** When your team members are struggling, offer help, but have an exit plan. Here are some statements and questions that will help you clarify that you are giving back ownership.

   - I'm happy to help you think this through, but you are still the lead on this.
   - Those are thoughts to consider. You can take it from here.
   - I'm here to back you up. What do you need from me as you lead this?

The Promise:

As a leader, people around you will constantly bring you problems that bait you into taking over. When you resist the bait, you allow people the dignity of completing their own work and solving their own problems. "Give the pen back," and people around you will grow in their capability and independence.

* Reference the Investor chapter for the "Give back the pen" and "Don't give me an A-W-K without an F-I-X" stories.

Use this worksheet to plan and reflect on your Multiplier Experiments.

1. Experiment Purpose

What problem are you trying to address?	What do you hope to accomplish?

2. Document Your Plan

When and where will you try this?	What might limit success?	What will you do to overcome these hurdles?

3. Establish Measures

How will you know if you've been successful?	How will you get feedback?

4. Evaluate Results

What happened?	What impact did you have on others?	What was accomplished?

5. Study Your Learning

What surprised you?	What could you do differently to improve your results?	How would you describe the return on your investment for this experiment?

6. Make Lasting Change

How will you make this part of your ongoing management practice?	When and where will you use this approach again?

We'd love to hear about your successes with this Multiplier Experiment. Visit MultiplierEffectBook.com to share your story.

A Multiplier of Multipliers

Multipliers invest in others in a way that builds independence. The independence they create in others allows them to invest over and over, becoming a serial Multiplier.

Shortly after the original book *Multipliers* came out, Liz received a short message on the book website. It simply said, "Accidental Diminisher seeking recovery and reform," and gave contact information. Of course, Liz couldn't resist calling to hear the story behind an inquiry so brief it appeared meant for transmission via Morse code. The voice on the other end of the phone belonged to a thoughtful, soft-spoken CEO named Rick who had founded a creative company that he scaled into a global services firm over 25 years. He said, "I've just read *Multipliers* and it struck a chord with me. I realized that I've spent most of my career as an Accidental Diminisher. I believe I am a Multiplier at heart, but all of my role models have been Diminishers. I have about 10 years of my career left. I'd like to go out as a Multiplier." His sincerity was obvious. He continued, "And I'd like to create a lot of other Multipliers inside this company in the process."

We have watched in awe as Rick and leaders like him have come to understand the ways they've accidentally diminished, become Multipliers, and build other Multipliers around them. To build a great product or program is a noble contribution. To build people who can go onto to build something great themselves, this is a legacy. This is what educators do.

When administrators operate as Micromanagers, they ensure things get done, but when Diminishers leave, things fall apart. When Multipliers leave, they leave a legacy.

End Notes

1. Name of the leader has been changed.
2. Roger Robinson, "London Olympics: 1908 & 1948," *Running Times*, May 8, 2012.
3. Name of the leader has been changed.
4. Name of the leader has been changed.

AT A GLANCE: THE INVESTOR

MICROMANAGERS jump in, give commands, and get results. They may get the job done, but they often get inferior results and create a leader-dependent organization. Micromanagers believe:

- Their team won't be able to figure it out without their involvement.

INVESTORS define ownership and expectations up front, shifting the burden of accountability onto others. They create an organization capable of delivering results independent of the leader. Investors believe:

- People perform at their best when they have natural responsibility and know someone is counting on them.

Three Practices of the Investor:

1. *Give others ownership*—Put other people in charge by definitively transferring responsibility.

2. *Provide backup*—Make sure people have the resources needed to deliver on their accountability. Do this by teaching, coaching, infusing means, and running interference.

3. *Hold people accountable*—Give the work back, never doing anything for your people that they can do for themselves.

Becoming an Investor:

1. Create a cycle of success by nurturing failure. Let others learn from their own mistakes instead of fixing things for them.

2. Put someone else in charge using the *Give 51% of the Vote Experiment*

3. Conduct the *Give It Back Experiment* to play the role of coach, rather than problem solver.

7

The Accidental Diminisher

Good intentions may do as much harm as malevolence if they lack understanding.

Albert Camus

The school was facing a critical application that would determine its status as a Blue Ribbon school, and the responsibility fell on Sally, a veteran principal. She loved analytical work and was drawn to anything that involved data, spreadsheets, and synthesis. She dove into the briefing documents to get a thorough understanding of the analysis that would need to get done. Realizing that the project was significant and needed a lot of further analysis, she decided to get her assistant principal involved.

Marcus was relatively new to his role (and to spreadsheet work), but he was smart, thorough, and insightful. She decided to hand the data analysis over to him, giving him full ownership. Sally wanted him to be successful, so she carefully planned the handoff. She met with him, reviewed the report specifications with him, told him he would be in charge, and laid out clear expectations for what needed to get done.

Sally then began working on other elements of the report and waited for Marcus to send the data analysis to her. When he hadn't sent it 2 days later, she suspected he was struggling and, wanting to help him, she sent him more instructions and suggested some categories to use for analyzing the qualitative data. Again, she didn't hear much from him. She stopped by his desk to see if he had finished it. He hadn't.

Knowing how conscientious Marcus was, Sally assumed he needed more help. She sat down and offered him support, "How can I be of help to you with this analysis?" When she didn't get a concrete response, she began offering suggestions, "Would it help if I gave you a quick tutorial on how to use the statistics functions in Excel? Or perhaps we can sit down together and go through the data elements?" Strangely, he didn't bite at any of the offers.

Sally was growing frustrated. Clearly Marcus needed help, but she couldn't figure out how to help him. Sally was about to offer to do the first set of analysis with him, but he started to speak before she could. Sally stopped talking and gave him her full attention, thrilled to finally learn what help he needed from her. He began tentatively but grew more confident as he said, "Sally, I think I could use . . . just a little less help from you."

Sally sheepishly acknowledged his message and that her attempt to assist might have been more of a hindrance than a help. She backed off and gave him the space he needed to figure it out on his own. And he did. This smart, capable, conscientious assistant principal delivered an analysis that was a vital contribution to the report that allowed this school to once again be awarded Blue Ribbon status.

Despite the best of intentions, this administrator had become an Accidental Diminisher. While her intent was to help, her help was a hindrance.

How might we, with the very best of intentions, have a diminishing impact on the people we lead? Can people be hindered by our honest attempts to help or teach or lead by example? Discovering the answer to this question might be the key to truly becoming a Multiplier to the people we lead.

What happens when an administrator is too quick with ideas and too swift with action? Or too supportive and helpful? Or just enthusiastic or optimistic? Surely these are character virtues—the kind taught in Sunday school or in business school. Indeed they are, but many popular management practices can lead us, subtly but surely, down the slippery slope to becoming an Accidental Diminisher.

The following are the most frequent ways that good managers, and truly good people, can end up having a diminishing impact on the people around them.

THE ACCIDENTAL DIMINISHER

Idea Guy

This type of leader is an innovative thinker and a veritable fountain of ideas that is sure to gush forth after he or she reads a great article, attends a conference, or has a great run. The Idea Guy bursts into the school office brimming with new ideas to share with colleagues.

These leaders don't necessarily think their ideas are superior. They simply believe that the more they toss around their ideas, the more they will spark ideas in others.

But what actually happens around an Idea Guy? At first he or she creates a great chase. As the leader serves up the idea du jour, others are intrigued and begin pursuing the idea, thinking, "Yes, we should create a new website!" or "Yes, let's create a survey to solicit parent views." However, as soon as they begin to make progress, there is another idea that flows forth, distracting them and sending them off on a new chase. The team ends up making a millimeter of progress in hundreds of directions. The great chase becomes a standstill as they realize that they always end up back at square one—*so why not just stay there?* As

they learn to stop acting on the leader's ideas, they also stop trying to come up with their own ideas. After all, if they actually need a new idea, they can just wait for the fountain to spew, pick up a new idea off the ground, and have a go at it.

If you are a fountain of ideas, don't be surprised if your team merely stands around waiting for the fountain to over-flow.

Always On

This is the dynamic, charismatic leader. This is the leader who is always engaged, always present, always energetic, and always has something to contribute and to say. Many of these leaders have been blessed with the gift of gab! They dart around their organization assuming their energy is infectious. Surely their energy will spark energy in others—woohoo! These leaders think the more they communicate their point of view, the more people will be wooed by it.

What actually happens when leaders are always on? As they expand like a gas consuming the available space around them, others suffocate. People shrink around these leaders, not only because they're oxygen deprived, but because these leaders are just plain exhausting. Soon people avoid making eye contact, having encounters with them thinking, *You're killing me with all this energy*. Reaction to their "woohoo" effect becomes, *Oh no, not again*. And all too often, thinking introverts get suppressed while action-oriented extroverts dominate.

What do people do to these leaders? Well, what do you do to the human being who lacks an "off" switch? Yes, you simply turn them off inside your head. You put them in the background; they become like white noise. Their endless spray of speech becomes muffled and sometimes completely unheard by the people they lead. Before long, they sound like the infamous teacher in the Peanuts cartoons: "Wuah wuah wuah wuah wuah wuah."

In her first year as a university-based career coach, Elise learned the lesson that confidence, not energy, is contagious.

> I was excited to be working with MBA students who most certainly had high career aspirations. Brimming with eagerness to get these students off on the right career footing, I carefully planned our first workshop together based on a video that describes how the difference between steam and water is only 1 degree.[1] This seemed like the perfect way to show students how that extra push in their search would separate the students who get *a job* from those who get their *dream job*. I hoped this would spur students to attack their job search with vigor.
>
> I kicked off the session with a dynamic and charismatic presentation. Yet the energy in the room was at an all-time low. It was early, so I ratcheted up the energy level only to find the students becoming even more disengaged. My high energy and their low energy combined to create a strange tension in the room. One student even said, "It almost felt like we were bullied by your charisma and energy." I had hoped

to sway people toward my coaching, but I suspected most people left the session swayed away. I realized that having confidence in each student was more powerful than any "woohoo" speech ever could be. I spent the rest of the semester listening, rebuilding relationships, and instilling confidence in my students.

Always On leaders think they are being big, but actually they become small, and they make everyone around them small, too. Energy isn't contagious. Attitude and confidence in others are. When the leader is always on, everyone else is always off.

Rescuer

This is the good manager and the decent person. The rescuer is the type of leader who doesn't like to see people struggle, make mistakes, or fail. So at the first sign of a problem, they jump in and help. They lend a hand, resolve a problem, and help people across the finish line. Incidentally, we find that this is the most common way educational leaders (and actually all managers in the corporate world) accidentally diminish.

The intention of Rescuers is noble. They want to see other people be successful; they desire to protect the reputation of the people who work for them. Because Rescuers interrupt a natural performance cycle, they starve people of vital learning they need to be successful. Furthermore, Rescuers create a vexing, and all too pervasive, performance disconnect because they deprive people of the feedback that comes from the natural consequences of mistakes. Employees see undeniable success while the manager sees failure and a gap to step in and close. You can hardly blame the employees for this delusion; after all, everywhere they turn, *I*s are getting dotted and *T*s are getting crossed. Their work always crosses the finish line on time, as they are helped by the invisible hand of the Rescuer.

When leaders play the role of Rescuer, they create dependency across their team. They become the Knight in Shining Armor while their team is relegated to play the Damsel in Distress and wait idly for the inevitable rescue.

If you love to help people who are struggling, consider a career in customer service (and help people find their lost luggage!), but you might want to stay out of leadership roles. When managers help too soon and too often, people around them become helpless. Sometimes we are most helpful when we don't help.

Pacesetter

Pacesetters are achievers who strive to improve the organization because they envision their school or district being capable of more. To build momentum, they personally set the standard for performance, for quality, for speed, and so on. They take the lead, set the pace, and expect that the people around them will notice, follow, and, of course, catch up to them.

What actually happens when the leader speeds out ahead? Do others pick up the pace or do they fall behind?

The effect is subtle. The leader is half right: People do take notice. They catch on, but rarely do they catch up. Instead of speeding up, they most often assume the role of spectator. After all, here's what they see: You're out in front, moving fast and working hard. It looks like a lot of work, so it must be either easy for you or just plain fun. They start to think, *Good show, boss! When you lap me next time, let me know if you need any help!*

While you are expecting your staff to speed up, they are actually slowing down or sitting down. Or perhaps, recognizing the growing gap between you and them, they simply give up.

Liz was taught how this works by a 7-year-old boy who was both a fast runner and a quick study.

My son Joshua loves to run, and for most of his second-grade year he insisted we race to the bus stop each day. Like any good mother, I understood the purpose of these races was to encourage his budding love of running, so I made sure to let him win or to make it a close, rousing competition.

But every now and then I would forget. I, too, love to run and enjoy the feeling of turning it on and crossing the finish line first (or maybe just not last). Joshua is my youngest child and the only child that I could still beat at a foot race. Fueled by some sudden vain ambition (AKA midlife crisis), I would take off running at full speed and easily beat him to the bus stop. As I would catch my breath and look back, I would see that he had stopped running and was now walking. This seemed strange because he loved to race! As he walked closer, I could see the look on his face was a muddle of disappointment and disapproval. When he arrived at the bus stop, he would shrug his shoulders and say indifferently, "I wasn't racing this time."

Every time I lost my head and raced out in front, creating a gap too big for him to close, the same scene ensued. He stopped running and began walking. And when he got to the bus stop, he again said, "I wasn't racing." He had learned that when he couldn't keep up, it was best to just let me win.

As leaders, sometimes the faster we run, the slower others walk. When leaders set the pace, they create spectators instead of followers.

Rapid Responder

And what about the leader who is quick to take action? Rapid Responders are leaders who prize agility and quick turnaround. They are quick to respond, troubleshoot problems, and make fast micro-decisions. We all know these people. They see a problem; they solve a problem. They see a mole; they whack a mole. An email doesn't last long in their inbox. They open, read, and resolve immediately. Their intent is noble. They want an agile, fast organization that can respond to the diverse needs of the stakeholders and community.

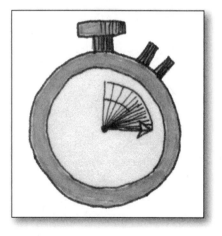

But what is the perspective from someone else's inbox? If you work for a Rapid Responder, you know the scene. You are sitting at your computer. You open an email sent to you and notice your boss is copied on it. As it falls in your area of responsibility, you are "on it." Reading it carefully, you contemplate the options. You realize you need more information, so you consult a colleague. When you come back to your desk to finish your reply, you get that sinking feeling that your boss may have responded in the interim. Saving your draft, you click on "get new mail." Frustrated, you discover that indeed she has! You delete your draft. A couple days later you open another email on a related issue. With a sigh of exasperation, you suspect your boss will jump on this one, too, and will have hit "send" before you can get the first two sentences written, so you close the email and do something else.

These leaders can also create activity traffic jams across their organization. Because they respond to problems and questions quickly, they release a lot of decisions into the workflow of their team. The roads become flooded with decisions and actions, people move at a crawl, and soon it is full-fledged gridlock.

These leaders move fast, but the people around them tend to move slowly.

Optimist

These are the positive, can-do managers who believe that everything is possible. They believe that most problems can be tackled with

hard work and the right mindset. They've read the research on the power of positive thinking and the incredible mental and physical benefits of optimism. They are "glass half-full" kind of folk.

They aren't necessarily cheerleaders; they just focus on what is possible and believe that the people around them (themselves included) *are smart and can figure it out.* So how could this possibility be diminishing?

Liz found out the answer to this question a couple years ago from a colleague who didn't find the optimistic approach nearly as assuring as she did.

A colleague and I were in the middle of a high-stakes research project where we had a small window of opportunity to write an article for a prestigious academic publication. To pull this off, we needed to complete some complex analysis, do a round of additional research, and actually write the article, all while working on several other projects and operating on a thin budget.

Having years of experience in the corporate world, where a given week involved juggling knives, pulling rabbits out of hats, and rubbing two nickels together to pay for it all, to me this seemed feasible and an interesting challenge. I enthusiastically attacked the project, providing leadership along the way to my more junior colleague. At one critical meeting, he turned to me and said, "Liz, I need you to stop saying that!" "Saying what?" I asked. He replied, "Saying that thing you always say: *'How hard can it be?'*" I looked puzzled. He explained, "You say that all the time. *'How hard can it be? We can do this. After all, how hard can it be?'*"

I could see his point emerging. While I was working for Oracle, a rapidly growing company, I had been thrown into management at the tender age of 24 and was told that I was now in charge of training for the entire company. A month into the job, they charged me with building a corporate university. After a year of figuring this out, and now just 25 years old, the management asked me to globalize Oracle University and make it operate in over 100 countries. Having never even been out of the United States, I secured a passport and flew to Europe to start there first. These formative experiences taught me that a team of smart, driven people could do almost anything. I learned to say to myself, "*I can do this. After all, how hard can it really be?*" This attitude (termed a "growth mindset" by Dr. Carol Dweck)[2] worked beautifully for me and many of my colleagues over the years.

My current colleague's voice reeled me back from my reflection: "Yes, *that* is what I need you to stop saying." "But why?" I probed. He paused and looked me straight in the eye and said, "Because what we are doing *is actually* really hard." After another deliberate pause he continued, "And I need you to acknowledge that."

He wasn't opposed to the idea that it was doable; he simply wanted me to acknowledge the reality of the challenge and recognize his struggle. He didn't want me glossing over the challenge with my coat of optimism. Having heard his sincere message, I looked at him squarely and acknowledged, "Yes, what we are doing *is* hard. It is really, really difficult. I suppose I just meant that we are really capable and I'm confident we'll figure it out." I could see the tension lifting. I assured him that I would do my best to stop saying "that thing." Meanwhile, in the back of my mind I told myself, "Sure, I can stop saying that. After all, *how hard can it be?*"

Is it possible that a can-do attitude that worked so well for you as teacher or in a previous role may actually work against you as a leader? When you play the role of the optimist, you undervalue the struggle the team is experiencing and the hard-fought learning and work. Your staff may wonder if you have lost your tether to reality and are lost in space. Or worse, you might be sending an unintentional message that mistakes and failure are not an option, after all, *how hard can it be?*

When the leader sees only the upside, it opens room for others to become preoccupied with the downside.

ARE YOU AN ACCIDENTAL DIMINISHER?

Having any of the above tendencies doesn't make you a Diminisher; it simply increases the likelihood that you will have a diminishing impact. That's the good news. The bad news is that when it does cause a diminishing impact, you are likely to be completely unaware and probably the last to know.

As a leader, how do you know whether you are having a diminishing effect, despite having the best of intentions? How do you increase your self-awareness?

Formulating and recording your own insights is a reasonable first step. As you read the various Accidental Diminisher profiles above, surely some resonated, giving you a sharp inkling or maybe even a pang of guilt. You can bring this vague suspicion into sharper focus by taking our online quiz, "Are You an Accidental Diminisher?" at MultiplierEffectBook.com. This 3-minute quiz provides additional structure to help you self-assess and analyze your potentially diminishing habits.

Then, go beyond self-assessment and consult the actual experts—the people you might be diminishing. These are the people who are the real customers of your leadership. The best way to get this unfiltered feedback is to use a 360 assessment (see MultiplierEffectBook.com), but you can also do it the old-fashioned way—by asking good, honest, face-to-face questions. Here are some questions you might use to elicit this feedback:

- How might I be shutting down the ideas and actions of others, despite having the best of intentions?
- What am I inadvertently doing that might be having a diminishing impact on others?

- How might my intentions be interpreted differently by others? What messages might my actions actually be conveying?
- What could I do differently?

A management team in the United Arab Emirates (UAE) taught Liz how easy, and important, this can be.

The best part about teaching leadership seminars in the UAE is seeing the Emirati men in their striking kanduras and gutras. These are the traditional robe and head cloths worn by men across most of the Middle East. These Emirati men look regal in their crisp white robes, as do the women in their black flowing abiyahs. The worst part about teaching there is wondering how badly I'm violating the strong cultural norms of the region.

On this particular trip, I am in Abu Dhabi conducting a full-day Multipliers workshop for the management team of a regional manufacturer. The management team is diverse, like much of the UAE population. The CEO is European and the rest of the team is a fusion of talent from the Middle East, Europe, and Asia.

As one might expect, teaching people to lead like Multipliers is best done by teaching like a Multiplier oneself. So I offer stretch challenges, hold debates, and ask lot of questions—big, provocative questions that prompt self-reflection and shift the burden of thinking to the leaders in the room. Today is no exception, but knowing the likelihood that I'm offending cultural norms, I keep a careful watch on the group's reaction in case I cross a line.

The group is delightfully engaged and enjoying the session. I asked each person to write down one way he or she might be accidentally diminishing. They did. I then asked them to share their insight with their colleagues at their table. They hesitated for a moment but then did. This is a huge relief because I suspect the exercise is challenging for a culture with such strong hierarchal norms. I am quietly relieved and sit down to gather a few thoughts. A couple minutes later, I look up and notice that the exercise is not proceeding as planned. People are getting up, moving around, and I see a swirl of white kanduras as people move to other tables. Immediately I assume that they are opting out of the exercise and are conducting other business instead. Concerned, I move closer to observe and then ask Khalid, a warm and articulate Emirati national, to help me understand what is happening. He responds, "We were sharing our own observations, but then we realized we really should be asking our colleagues to tell us how we are accidentally diminishing. So we are moving into new groups so we can get feedback from the people we work with most closely." I watch in fascination as individuals move around the room, scurrying to find a small group or partner who can give them honest feedback.

This leadership team understood that self-awareness as a leader comes from understanding the perspectives of those we lead and serve. Our learning can start with our own insight, but it can't end there. To become intentional Multipliers, we must understand how our best intentions can be translated and received differently by others.

Leading with Intention

Leading with intention starts with understanding how your natural tendencies can take you down the wrong path. The next step is then finding ways to identify these tendencies when they happen, replacing them with better practices or simple workarounds.

The following chart offers strategies to develop these new practices. You might try one of the *Multiplier Experiments* (found at the end of Chapters 2–6). Or you might try a simple workaround that you can use in the moment. These include abiding by a simple rule of thumb like *Wait 24 hours before replying to emails if you want others to respond* or creating a filter like *If you don't want anyone to take action on this idea, don't share it yet*. As one aspiring Multiplier said, "I can't control the ideas that pop into my head, but I can control the ones that come out of my mouth."

Do Less and Challenge More

Becoming a Multiplier often starts with becoming less of a Diminisher. And this often means doing less: less talking, less responding, less convincing, and less rescuing of others who need to struggle and learn for themselves. By doing less, we can become more of a Multiplier.

ACCIDENTAL DIMINISHER REPLACEMENT PRACTICES

Accidental Diminisher Profile	Multiplier Experiment	Page	Simple Workaround
Idea Guy	Extreme Questions	85	*Create a Holding Tank.* Before you share a new idea, stop and ask yourself if you want the people who work for you to take action on it—right now. If not, hold off sharing it, and put it into a holding tank in your brain or on a piece of paper.
Always On	Play Fewer Chips Give 51% of the Vote	60 126	*Say It Just Once.* When we are most excited, we tend to repeat ourselves and re-explain for emphasis, hoping to get positive reactions from our colleagues. Avoid overcontributing by saying the important things just once, and create a reason for others to chime in and build on the idea.
Rescuer	Make Space for Mistakes Give it Back	62 128	*Ask for Their "F-I-X".* When someone brings you a problem or signals a need for help, remind yourself that he or she probably already has a solution. Ask, "How do you think we should solve it?"
Pacesetter	Give 51% of the Vote	126	*Stay Within Sight.* If you have a tendency to pull out ahead, remind yourself to stay within sight so people don't give up or get lost. Don't get more than two to three car lengths ahead of the pack; don't go around a corner. Stay within distance that someone could realistically catch up.
Rapid Responder	Extreme Questions Make a Debate	85 107	*Set a Mandatory Waiting Period.* Wait 24 (or however many) hours before responding to any email if someone else should be responding. Give that person the first right of response.
Optimist	Make Space for Mistakes Talk Up Your Mistakes	62 64	*Signal the Struggle.* Before offering your boundless enthusiasm, start by acknowledging how hard the work is. Let people know, "What I am asking you to do is hard. I'm not sure it's been done before. Success isn't guaranteed." With that said, express your belief in them and what is possible.

Doing less to achieve more is one of many examples where counterintuition is more instructive than intuition. When no one else is speaking up, the compelling inclination is to jump in and fill the void. We become a greater Multiplier when we learn to hold back and allow silence to draw in others. When we feel the need to be big, let it be a signal that we need to be small and dispense our views in small but intense doses. And when our instincts tell us to help, we might need to help less.

Becoming a Multiplier requires us to understand how our most noble intentions can have a diminishing effect, sometimes deeply so. Reinhold Niebuhr, the American theologian, said, "All human sin seems so much worse in its consequences than in its intentions." Likewise, while leaders view their own leadership through the lens of their good intentions, their staff perceive that same behavior only by its consequences—the consequences on them and the students they serve.

By learning to do less and challenge more, we can transform from being the Accidental Diminisher to the Intentional Multiplier.

End Notes

1. Full video can be found at http://www.youtube.com/watch?v=BLtMem BHbXo.

2. Carol Dweck, *Mindset: The New Psychology of Success* (New York: Random House, 2006).

AT A GLANCE: THE ACCIDENTAL DIMINISHER

THE ACCIDENTAL DIMINISHER is the well-intended leader, often following popular management practices, who subtly and, completely unaware, shuts down the intelligence of others.

THE MOST FREQUENT ACCIDENTAL DIMINISHER TENDENCIES

Tendency	Intention	Outcome	Replacement or Multiplier Experiment
Idea Guy	For their ideas to stimulate ideas in others	They overwhelm others, who either shut down or spend time chasing the idea du jour.	Create a Holding Tank *Extreme Questions*
Always On	To create infectious energy and share their point of view	They consume all the space, and other people tune them out.	Say It Just Once *Play Fewer Chips* *Give 51% of the Vote*
Rescuer	To ensure people are successful and to protect their reputation	Their people become dependent on them, which weakens their reputation.	Ask for Their "F-I-X" *Make Space for Mistakes* *Give It Back*
Pacesetter	To set a high standard for quality or a pace	Other people become spectators or give up when they can't keep up.	Stay Within Sight *Give 51% of the Vote*
Rapid Responder	To keep their organization moving fast	They move fast, but their organization moves slowly because there is a traffic jam of too many decisions or changes.	Set a Mandatory Waiting Period *Extreme Questions* *Make a Debate*
Optimist	To create a belief that the team can do it	People wonder if they appreciate the struggle and the possibility of failure.	Signal the Struggle *Make Space for Mistakes* *Talk Up Your Mistakes*

LEADING WITH INTENTION allows a leader to understand how his or her natural tendencies become barriers to accessing intelligence.

1. Identify when these tendencies happen, and replace them with better practices.

2. Bring clarity to your observations by taking our online quiz, "Are You an Accidental Diminisher?" The quiz can be found at MultiplierEffectBook.com

3. Use your results and ask others. Adjust. Continue on your journey.

8

Becoming
a Multiplier School

*Your present circumstances don't determine where you can go;
they merely determine where you start.*

Nido Qubein

At this point, like many other readers, you're probably wondering, what could this look like for me, in my school? They all make it look so easy, how can I possibly lead this way? Is it conceivable for me to shed some of my Accidental Diminisher tendencies? If I can, what might it look like and what will I miss from the old days? Finally, how will I stick with it? We find these are nearly universal observations and questions that are coupled with a great aspiration. Most of us have a genuine desire, but are often overwhelmed by the standard of the Multiplier and the apparent magnitude of the task of becoming one. And if we are overwhelmed at the idea as an individual, what does that mean for the notion of becoming a Multiplier school?

Having observed and talked to hundreds of educators, we recognize why learning to lead like a Multiplier can feel overwhelming. For a start, many national and educational cultures lean to the

Diminisher side; Multiplier leadership isn't often the norm. The path of least resistance is frequently the path of the Diminisher. And while we appreciate the challenge, we also have worked with educational leaders who have grown, become Multipliers, and realized the benefits of this approach. It is not hard to be a Multiplier, but it is definitely easier to fall into the traps of leading like a Diminisher.

Let's examine the experiences of a few of the educational leaders who have ventured down the path of leading themselves and their schools to be more like Multipliers.

Distributing Leadership

What would you be thinking if a copy of *Multipliers* landed in your mailbox, *before* you set foot on campus at the school where you just accepted a leadership position? Uncertainty? Worry? Intrigue? Is this a hint? It's probably a combination of those thoughts, coupled with curiosity.

Well, that's just what happened when Nick Dennis signed on as the assistant principal at the Berkhamsted School for Boys. Mark Steed, introduced earlier, was the principal whose straightforward act of putting a book in the mail sparked aspirations of Multiplier leadership throughout the school. From Nick's perspective, this was a disciplined cultural on-boarding, one that would allow him to shape his leadership style in a positive way. Nick said, "Giving ownership and making everyone feel smart is integral to what we do. The best teachers are already doing this." Nick and his colleagues began experimenting, looking to fuel growth and academic improvement within their respective areas.

When Mark became principal of the Berkhamsted Schools Group in September 2008, he recognized the impossibility of centrally leading a school of its large size, breaking a long tradition. In the original *Multipliers*, Mark found a model to describe his vision of leadership, one of distributed leadership, where responsibility is shared across levels, with as many people as possible. By letting go and letting others take the lead, Berkhamsted has been able to tackle projects previously seen as impossible.

Now, assignments are rarely handed down; rather, staff members are encouraged to identify and undertake any project that supports one of five school objectives. The once sterile, dry update meetings have turned into hugely successful show-and-tell sessions. Staff members are more engaged, working on initiatives of their choosing, while at the same time held accountable to deliver results. Leaders can be found saying, "I don't mind how you do it, who you work with, or how you organize the people below you." As a result of this Investor mindset, they have seen programs, such as e-learning, taken to the next level.

The leadership team looks out on their staff with a renewed sense of excitement, recognizing a sea of intelligence ready to be harnessed and utilized. An important revelation for the school was this: The leaders at Berkhamsted don't see Multiplier leadership as a way to work any less, but they do see themselves doing a different job than before. This redefined role is one that allows each to focus on the issues that matter most, rather than the issue of the moment.

Going Big, Going Small

Jim Vangerud, a Minnesota middle school math department chair and a self-proclaimed talking guy, said, "I don't tell you the time. I tell you how to make the watch in detail." This observation caused him to wonder how much shorter meetings would be without him controlling the airwaves and consuming so much airtime. He decided to try an extreme form of the *Play Fewer Chips Experiment* in an upcoming professional development committee meeting and assigned himself exactly zero poker chips. Afterward, a surprised colleague sincerely asked, "You didn't say a word. Are you okay?" Jim responded by describing his experiment and noting that the meeting was 50% shorter when he didn't speak. Having sized up his oversized contribution, Jim continued with the *Play Fewer Chips Experiment* and actually played his chips, but did so carefully, dispensing his ideas in much smaller doses. He noticed contributions from a broader selection of the team and a sudden absence in the trivial issues. His experimentation helped him find the balance between going big and going small, creating space for more voices to be heard.

Making A Debate

It was the fall of 2012, with the Chicago teacher strike imminent. Cherie Novak, principal at Robert Fulton Elementary, a turnaround school, was invited to take a Multiplier Experiment. She selected the

Make a Debate Experiment because she wanted to challenge herself, very aware of her own decision-making tendencies. What she didn't know was that the experiment can be a bit risky absent some form of coaching or the Community Builder chapter, which hadn't yet been published. She had neither.

But she had been grappling with an important decision. The Instructional Leadership Team, a partnership between teachers and principals, believed that teachers benefit tremendously from having a coach. Nearly one-third of the way through the year, they considered changing the teacher-coach pairs to offer a new perspective. Cherie had a strong opinion, but knew she couldn't make the decision on her own.

In Cherie's eyes, two elements made this the perfect opportunity to experiment with debate. First, she confessed that she typically went into a debate knowing the answer she wanted people to pick, fully thinking she knew what was best for the school as a whole, and then tried to win the argument. Second, this question presented two clear options: (a) keep the same coaches or (b) reassign coaches? Cherie walked into the debate ready; she had her notes, an opening question, a position, data, and a plan for how to decide.

She framed the debate, probed, and drove to a conclusion: reassign coaches. Next an informed team went straight to implementation. Afterward, Cherie said, "Debate makes a lot of sense. It makes a more well-informed decision, but it doesn't make the decision any easier." She recognized that despite her team's characteristic willingness to challenge her on issues, people sometimes concede prematurely, due to the voice of a strong, well-intended leader. This method of debate obliges people to weigh in before the decision is made, creating transparency and a community of decision owners.

As Robert Fulton Elementary faces a difficult budget cut, Cherie plans to use debate to drive a sound decision based on data, not emotion. She envisions a community rallying to overcome a difficult cut in resources, rather than a team saying, "It's going to be sad without so and so around."

As an educator you already know how to lead like a Multiplier. It is at the core of what you do to grow future generations. Many of us operated like Multipliers in the classroom, but having moved into a leadership or administrative position, we assumed our jobs required a new approach. But even if we didn't teach like Multipliers, one need only watch a 5-year-old child for 5 minutes to remember that curiosity, asking questions, and a willingness to challenge and debate come naturally to people. These skills are innate in us, but may be lying dormant.

What will it take for us to awaken these native skills both in ourselves and in other leaders? We'll start by offering strategies, examples, and tools to help you lead more like a Multiplier individually. We'll then explore how you can build a Multiplier culture across a school, a district, or an entire educational community.

BECOMING A MULTIPLIER

Deciding to shift your style toward Multiplier leadership is likely the most difficult part of your journey. But once you've developed the resolve, how can you make it a reality? Based on our observations studying dozens of educational leaders who have successfully made the shift, we offer four strategies to help you consistently lead like a Multiplier.

1. Get Feedback

Can you imagine the frustration of rushing down a path—where you experiment, attempting to lead more like a Multiplier—only to find a staff confused and wondering why you've made the changes you have, rather than others? How many steps do you want to take before you figure out the most efficient and effective route to Multiplier leadership?

Here are three options that will give you insights and help you plan your path.

1. *Take the "Are You an Accidental Diminisher?"* quiz at MultiplierEffectBook.com Have fun with a short self-assessment to get you pointed in the right direction.

2. *Ask your colleagues.* Find three colleagues who can share the ways in which you might be an unintentional roadblock rather than a gateway. Make it a safe environment by sharing your purpose, and seek out individuals who are likely to be sincere and forthright. Use the questions in Chapter 7, pages 142–143, to get the conversation started.

3. *Take a formal assessment.* Use a formal assessment like the Utilization Index, a "3-minute 360," asking two questions to

find out how much intelligence you are accessing in the people with whom you work. You might also consider taking a Multiplier 360, which offers a full analysis of Multiplier-Diminisher behaviors and allows you to quickly access a baseline across the Multiplier model. See MultiplierEffectBook.com for a sample of these assessment tools.

Whether you choose a self-assessment, ask your colleagues, or take a formal assessment to point yourself in the right direction, taking the time to understand what you learn can allow you to leverage each effort you take, minimizing disappointment and maximizing impact.

2. Establish Singular Focus

You will make the most progress on your journey to becoming a Multiplier if you establish a singular focus. Here, we can learn from the efforts of Benjamin Franklin,[1] a man known for his curiosity and interest in self-improvement. Franklin attempted one of his greatest challenges: "to arrive at moral perfection." He found the undertaking to be overwhelming, as he faced disappointing results and concluded that he needed a new approach. He began by settling on a list of 13 virtues but, more important, decided a measured approach—mastering one virtue before proceeding to the next—would provide the highest likelihood of success. The mere act of prioritizing and working toward mastery enabled Franklin to manage his quest for perfection. Admittedly, he never reached it, but he did say, "Yet I was, by the [endeavour], a better and a happier man than I otherwise should have been if I had not attempted it."

There are five disciplines—Talent Finder, Liberator, Challenger, Community Builder, and Investor—that distinguish Multipliers. Taking time to prioritize each step provides you with the focus you will need to achieve lasting results. Your personal circumstances, abilities, and interests will define your particular order. For example, if you are an administrator or teacher leader who is Always On, you might initially focus on the Liberator discipline, with a goal of talking less to give people more space to respond. You might then focus on the Challenger discipline, with the goal of asking more interesting questions to provoke deeper thinking and dialogue.

We recommend you target one area at a time, just as Franklin did, saving yourself from the disappointment of attempting all and mastering none. The following chart can help you establish your primary focus.

Multiplier Discipline	Multiplier Practices	Priority (1-5)	Why?
Talent Finder Attract talented people and use them at their highest point of contribution.	1. Scout out diverse intelligence. 2. Find people's native genius. 3. Utilize people at their fullest.		
Liberator Create an intense environment that requires people's best thinking and work.	1. Offer choice and space for others to contribute. 2. Demand people's best work. 3. Generate rapid learning cycles.		
Challenger Define an opportunity that causes people to stretch.	1. Ask provocative questions to guide discovery. 2. Lay down a challenge. 3. Generate belief in what's possible.		
Community Builder Drive sound decisions by constructing debate and decision-making forums.	1. Frame the issue. 2. Spark debate. 3. Drive a transparent decision.		
Investor Give other people the ownership for results and invests in their success.	1. Give others ownership. 2. Provide backup. 3. Hold people accountable.		

Without clarity of focus, it is all too common for motivated learners to establish an ambitious personal development agenda fraught with hyped expectations that they can't measure up to. They may attempt to relaunch their development plan, but these efforts typically end in defeat. Without a singular focus, we create a frustrating cycle we call "failure to launch," depicted on the next page.

Which practice will be most helpful for you to address first? How can planning your journey allow you to see lasting results? Add structure and order to your approach to find your way to success.

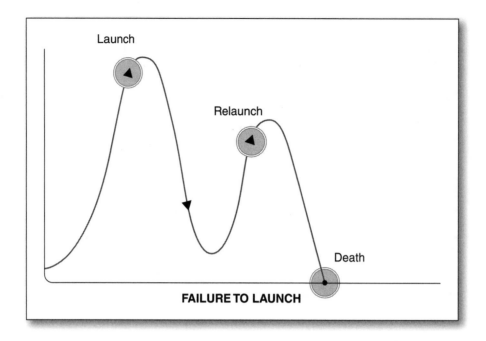

3. Create a Success Cycle

With a clear focus, begin building a pattern of small successful experiments that, in turn, will generate energy to fuel the next big step. You might find that, after a number of small wins, you experience a sudden acceleration as the small successes add up and begin to multiply and as others take notice.

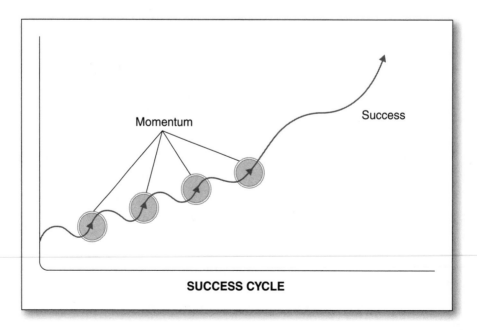

The following is a sample development plan, which you can use to build this momentum. Having targeted one Multiplier discipline, select the level that will give you the right amount of stretch. You might think of it as improving short-term, medium-term, and long-term ability to lead like a Multiplier through stretching your own comfort zone.

SAMPLE MULTIPLIER DEVELOPMENT PLANS

	More Comfortable	Moderately Comfortable	Less Comfortable
Talent Finder	Genius watch and document the projects you see people naturally select, including yourself	Try the *Name the Genius* Experiment for individuals on your team	Try the *Name the Genius* Experiment across an entire team
Liberator	Actively identify meetings where you tend to talk a lot and write down the purpose of the meeting, along with your role	Try the *Play Fewer Chips* Experiment	Begin to extract yourself from meetings
Challenger	Elicit ideas using *Extreme Questions* for 5 minutes	Elicit ideas using *Extreme Questions* for 1-3 hours	Try the *Lay a Concrete Challenge* Experiment
Community Builder	Seek out opinions from those who don't readily speak up	Use the Shared Inquiry method from Junior Great Books (see page 106) to lead a basic debate	Try the *Make a Debate* Experiment
Investor	Identify areas where you tend to take over on projects; identify what triggers you to take over	Try the *Give It Back* Experiment	Try the *Give 51% of the Vote* Experiment

Select the option that allows you to find your natural rhythm as you experiment with each practice, individually, according to your particular plan. You may find it helpful to see how one principal we studied created a virtuous cycle of success by focusing initially on the Liberator discipline and then moving on to Challenger.

In September 2010, after 5 years as the vice principal of Belvoir High School, in the United Kingdom, Paul Ainsworth became the interim principal. Suddenly, he found himself becoming the person people came to for answers—a common expectation of leaders. Paul found himself leading strategy meetings that quickly degenerated into briefings. The limitation of this briefing-style meeting became even more apparent when he noticed an excellent senior leader resist speaking in such a forum, but when Paul spoke to her individually, she contributed high-quality guidance.

Having recently read the original *Multipliers*, Paul began to challenge himself with questions. He wondered, "How might I, accidentally, be getting in the way of my team? How can I convince my team their input is valued?" He concluded that offering his ideas was preventing others from having a voice. Recognizing himself as the leader who is Always On, Paul decided to focus on becoming more of a Liberator and give his team more time and space to offer their ideas.

He started small. For half a term he resolved to never give a solution to the presenting problem; instead he would access the wisdom of the group. Over time, he got even more precise in his liberating approach. In advance of each meeting, he would develop a strategy to draw out some of the more reserved voices, noting whose input he would seek first. Very quickly he noticed results, hearing more voices. But Paul wasn't the only one to detect a change; his assistant remarked that she not only heard from the more reserved staff, but she saw team members participate earlier than usual.

Once the team started sharing openly, the meetings went from constant firefighting to strategy building. And they even noticed that this new environment neutralized the negative influences of any Diminishers in attendance. Having liberated his staff, Paul elected to shift his focus to the Challenger practice. Recognizing the deep experience and background of his team members, he began asking, "Have you seen this problem before? If so, what worked and what didn't? What do you think the solution is?" Then, each new solution would be passed to a different team member to see if he or she could improve on the solution—a form of on-the-spot coaching. At times, Paul found it hard to hold back his own ideas.

But he recognized that the greater value he offered was to reframe the problem or question, rather than present a solution.

Initially yielding to the pressures that come with the title of *leader*, and newly appointed on top of that, Paul made an important first step: acknowledging how his behaviors limited the organization. Rather than attempt a complete overhaul, he made small, but deliberate, shifts to extract the genius within Belvoir. What small shifts would allow you to make great gains? How might limiting your scope yield greater success? Carefully concentrating your efforts allows you and your team to lead more like Multipliers.

4. Create a Multipliers Learning Network

Making sustained behavior change, even the slightest bit, is hard work. Having support, encouragement, and insights from others taking on a similar endeavor will help you sustain your efforts and process your learning. Creating a Multipliers learning network can provide tremendous support as you tackle one of the most difficult challenges of your career: making lasting sustainable leadership change. One of our workshop participants, an urban high school principal, helped us see how a Multiplier community can provide support on the journey. He said, "I would like to think I'm leading like a Multiplier, but it would be nice to have a 'thinking partner' to help me along the way."

As you strengthen your own leadership, as well as others in your learning network, you are likely to find strength in numbers and notice that your efforts to lead like a Multiplier can be amplified or thwarted based on the larger school or district culture you are operating in. You might find yourself posing a new question. Instead of asking, "How can I become more of a Multiplier?" you might begin to ask, "How do we become a Multiplier school?"

BECOMING A MULTIPLIER SCHOOL

We are inspired and encouraged by the individuals, schools, and districts that have shared the wide-reaching impact of their Multiplier Experiments, including successes and obstacles. Each school started with someone's belief that becoming more of a Multiplier leader would create a cascade through the building and district. Let's see what this looked like in two school districts, one in Minnesota and the other in California, each with a bold vision.

Across the Board

In 2011, under the leadership of superintendent Dr. James Bauck, leaders in the Eastern Carver County School District in Minnesota were intrigued by the ideas in *Multipliers* and presented them as a leadership study. The initial group was inspired to implement the concepts across the 16 schools that comprise the district, from kindergarten centers through the high schools. As Dr. Bauck said, "I don't like reading books without making it practical and implementing something. If we are going to do this, we are going to spend some time on it." The group then organized a learning community that would meet monthly. Dr. Bauck posed two big questions: (1) How could we apply these principles in our day-to-day leadership? and (2) How will you use these ideas in the next 4 weeks to make a difference in your school? Dr. Bauck stepped back and let the leadership team take over.

Initially some teachers thought the book was an "administrative" read, but leaders and teachers alike quickly began to see the link between Multiplier leadership and the practices of the very best teachers, and they worked together to implement the ideas. These conversations were the spark that tapped in to talent such as Megan, from Pioneer Ridge Middle School, whose native genius led to the success of the community race, and middle school math teacher Jim Vangerud, who put the *Play Fewer Chips Experiment* to the test. Here are two more examples of Multiplier leadership in action in the Eastern Carver district.

Rekindling Genius: Sheryl Hough, Chaska Middle School West principal, was faced with a challenge: Implement a building-wide reading initiative, while the reading specialists were cut from full- to part-time. She not only found a way to implement the program, but she rekindled the genius of a master reading teacher. Sheryl got the idea that this teacher could present at each monthly staff meeting, sharing reading strategies that each teacher, regardless of subject, could use in the classroom. The staff embraced the techniques, getting creative with their own lessons and having fun at the same time. And the reading teacher regained use of a native genius that had been on the shelf, giving her greater confidence. Tapping into a native genius, growth was woven through each level—individual, teacher, and student.

From Answers to Questions: Jim Bach, principal of Chaska Middle School East, reflected, "*Multipliers* has helped me listen more." He has found it difficult, though, noting that people often look to the principal for the answers. He helps himself resist the temptation to provide answers by writing LISTEN on the page in front of him and asking questions to clarify.

These "pockets of brilliance," as they were called by Superintendent Bauck, were spotlighted in monthly learning community meetings, in which these aspiring Multipliers shared their experiences and built on each other's learning and successes. Some of the learning community members inevitably dropped out as the school year progressed, citing that all-too-common problem that they already had too much to do. However, the majority of teachers and leaders in this community recognized that Multiplier leadership isn't something you *do*; rather, it is a fundamental shift in *how* you do something. So they were able to overcome the natural barriers associated with taking on something new. Soon these pockets of brilliance became larger swaths of genius-in-action as the practices spread across the board and across the district.

Which of your day-to-day behaviors can you reimagine as a Multiplier? How might using a different approach to a common task yield a new outcome?

A Shared Vocabulary

Alyssa Gallagher, assistant superintendent of curriculum and instruction for the Los Altos School District, stumbled onto the Multipliers principles just as her district had undertaken a massive effort to revolutionize learning for all students. The *Multipliers* book offered her and superintendent Jeff Baier a chance to strengthen their leadership team and more deeply engage all teachers and staff in the challenge. They scheduled a Multipliers workshop for an upcoming administration meeting, with each principal and administrator reading the book in advance. In this session, they explored the Multiplier Effect and their Accidental Diminisher tendencies, and then dove into the art of asking great questions. At the conclusion of the workshop, each principal and district leader chose one of the Multiplier Experiments to conduct at his or her school during the next month.

After this first session, they discovered the power of simply putting a name on the way they had sought to operate as a district over the last 2 years. Administrators and principals learned the language of Multipliers, referencing and embracing it to drive deeper discussions with their staff. They then shared the results of their Multiplier Experiments as a district leadership team. Having a shared vocabulary also allowed the team to keep the learning active and weave the Multiplier concepts into their existing meetings and conversations. They used the terminology to consciously reframe the work they were already doing, asking questions such as "How can we solve this problem by asking the right questions?" and "How about debating this issue?"

Perhaps the greatest value of this new shared vocabulary was the platform it provided for giving each other gentle and good-spirited feedback. The principals began publicly identifying their own Accidental Diminisher tendencies, confessing to be a Rescuer or Rapid Responder. Their colleagues could easily identify and then offer suggested workarounds and coaching. One principal utilized the open block of time in a staff meeting to seek coaching from his peers. He described the problem that needed to be solved and said, "I'm wondering if my natural inclination is actually the most effective way?" The group helped him reframe his approach, and 2 weeks later he reported how the art of asking questions had altered the interaction with his team and positively affected the outcome.

How much further could you take your current strategy, school, or district simply by introducing a common leadership language? How could Multipliers coaching their peers influence the interactions across your school or district? As you commit to learn together, you can create a shared vocabulary that allows your team to open up, take risks, and grow into Multipliers.

Here are six steps we have seen work consistently across schools and districts. You may consider one of these as you create a Multiplier school or district.

1. *Introduce the Multiplier concepts.* Use the Chapter 1 summary on page 18 to seed the idea and plant the shared vocabulary. Then watch Multiplier leadership take root.

2. *Run a pilot.* Run an experiment with a small group of teachers, administrators, or students to create a success cycle.

3. *Host a school, district, or even community book read.* Create your own discussion questions, or use our book discussion guide found online at MultiplierEffectBook.com

4. *Keep the conversation alive.* Make a conscious effort to weave the concepts into your regularly scheduled meetings. Ask yourself, "How does asking questions apply to the problems we are solving?"

5. *Create a site-specific Multiplier learning network.* Tap into the experiences, and genius, of others by building a local Multipliers learning network, creating an opportunity for Multipliers to coach aspiring Multipliers. Remind this group to tap into the global community of aspiring Multipliers by visiting MultiplierEffectBook.com

6. *Reach out to The Wiseman Group.* Challenge us to see how we can support your development plan.

BECOMING A MULTIPLIER COMMUNITY

As individual deans, superintendents, principals, and teacher leaders work to build Multiplier schools, surely we will see hotspots where leaders, teachers, and students contribute at their fullest. We might even witness a new pattern of leadership emerging through this patchwork of individual efforts. However, what might happen if, instead of an organic, grassroots approach, national leaders called for a shift in leadership across a community of schools or across an entire industry? Could a Multiplier model of leadership help an entire industry or professional field tackle its toughest problems? Let's look at one such forerunner calling for a new model of leadership in the nexus of two of the biggest challenges facing the United States: healthcare and education.

On November 4, 2012, the weekend before the U.S. national elections, with a nation sharply divided along partisan lines, with impending healthcare reform legislation teetering between repeal and enactment, 4,000 medical education leaders in the American Association of Medical Colleges (AAMC) gathered in the Moscone Center in San Francisco for their annual conference. The group represented more than 150 medical schools in the United States and Canada, and the associated faculty, students, and resident physicians. The questions on everyone's mind were: *Will Obamacare (the Patient Care and Affordable Care Act) be repealed? Will the gridlock in Washington, D.C., ever end?* No one knew. The only thing every leader at the conference was certain about was that their medical schools and hospitals would be expected to provide more services and would be paid less for doing so.

Dr. Darrell Kirch, MD, president and CEO of the AAMC (and former psychiatrist, neuroscientist, and dean of medicine), took the stand for his keynote address titled "From Moses to Multipliers."[2] Dr. Kirch called for a new vision of leadership at the nation's medical schools and teaching hospitals that would multiply "the intelligence, creativity, and commitment of our faculty, students, residents, and institutional leaders . . . to create a sustainable future for academic medicine . . . and resolve the national problems we have been avoiding." Kirch noted that the search process in academic medicine traditionally seeks that "one leader with special knowledge to be the 'sage at the top,'" just as Clotaire Rapaille, author of *The Culture Code*, says our nation elects a "Moses" figure to lead as president. Waiting for a great leader seems hardwired into our culture.

"But today, I want to offer an alternative view," continued Dr. Kirch. "Perhaps we serve our nation and our institutions poorly by seeking a Moses[3] figure to lead us. Today, we need a new kind of leadership. What we need now is not a Moses, but a Multiplier." Citing the book *Multipliers*, Kirch described Multipliers as "leaders who unleash others' full potential and empower the broader problem-solving abilities of the entire organization. They invoke each person's unique intelligence and create an atmosphere of genius—innovation, productive effort, and collective intelligence."

Dr. Kirch then painted a picture of Multiplier leadership across our nation's medical schools and hospitals: "With nearly two million exceptionally talented and committed individuals, imagine what we could accomplish if more of us began to work as Multipliers. What creativity and innovation could be unleashed? What problems could be solved? Most important, what progress could we make toward improving the health of those we are privileged to serve? In our hierarchical world of medicine, moving from the Moses to the Multiplier model of leadership could be the game changer."

Dr. Kirch's call for a new model of leadership wasn't a future fantasy or a last-minute attempt to write a compelling speech. He had been seeing signs of Multipliers emerging at all levels in the medical schools and teaching hospitals he had visited. And his vision was the outcome of a thoughtful, collective effort across the AAMC over the previous year to articulate a new model of medical leadership and to provide the development programs to translate this model into a reality. This effort, led by Dr. Kevin Grigsby, had produced programs for new department chairs and deans to help them address their most pressing strategic challenges by "being and acting" in ways that multiply the leadership potential of the talented and committed people in their organizations. And they didn't stop with existing leaders. They extended these programs for individuals aspiring to become leaders.

After announcing these programs, Dr. Kirch concluded, "I think we are finally acknowledging that leadership no longer represents a special gift or power held by a select few. Instead, it is a relationship between committed people. It becomes an opportunity for all of us at any level."

Dr. Kirch could see that we not only need more Multipliers, we need Multiplier leadership across an entire professional community. We must all prepare for a future in which we do more with less. We must lead this transformation from within by harnessing the intelligence, creativity, and commitment of the faculty, students, and leaders in our educational institutions.

Could our medical schools deliver not only brilliant physicians who can treat illness but also a system of medical professionals to prevent illness across an entire population? Could our elementary and secondary schools do the same and improve student achievement while operating on tighter budgets?

In vital, enabling industries like healthcare and education, we need Multipliers across the entire community. It will take a shift in mindset and behavior to have a widespread impact.

GENIUS OR GENIUS MAKER?

When Philippe Petit illegally connected a tightrope wire between the 1,368-foot Twin Towers in New York City, he still had the chance to change his mind. The moment of truth came later, when he stood with one foot still on the building and another on the wire in front of him. The wire was bouncing up and down from the airflow between the buildings. His weight was still on his back leg. Petit described that critical moment as he stood on the edge overlooking the chasm. He reflected, "I had to make a decision of shifting my weight from one foot anchored to the building to the foot anchored on the wire. Something I could not resist called me [out] on that cable." He shifted his weight and took the first step.[4]

At the conclusion of this book, you may feel like Petit, with one foot anchored to the building of the status quo and the other anchored to the wire of change. You can remove your foot from the wire, lean back, and continue to lead the way you have in the past. Or you can shift your weight onto the wire and lead more like a Multiplier. Inertia will keep you on the building where it is comfortable and safe. But for many of us there is also a force pulling us out onto the wire and to a more impactful and fulfilling way of leading others. Will you shift your weight?

Consider some of the leaders who have made it across:

- Jeff Jones, Kootenay Lake superintendent, handed problems back to his district, through conversation and transparency, and in return received their involvement and support, setting the example throughout the district and causing one principal to say, "What Jeff did in the district, I am now doing in my school."
- Linda Aceves, Santa Clara County chief academic officer, built the capacity of district administrators and teachers using thought-provoking questions and, more important, gave them the time and safety to come up with their answers themselves.
- Brian Pepper, Heather Park Middle School principal, was known for taking a seat at the back of the room during staff meetings and providing safety and structure to allow all staff voices to be heard and valued. His insistence on offering insights and questions, from the back of the room, is long remembered as one of the many ways he shined a spotlight on his teachers.

These are just three leaders who are leading like Multipliers. You can be one, too. Join our Multipliers learning network to ask questions, learn from others who have made the shift, and share your own story.

Leading like a Multiplier is a choice we encounter daily or perhaps in every moment. What assumptions are driving the choices you make? And how will these choices affect what the people around you become? Is it possible that the choice you make about how you lead can impact not just your team, or even your immediate sphere of influence, but generations to come? A single Accidental Diminisher turned Multiplier could have a profound and far-reaching impact in a world where the challenges are so great and our full intelligence underutilized.

A Shifting World

Upon seeing the original Multipliers research, Liz's much admired and influential mentor Dr. CK Prahalad responded, "This is a really important idea because the critical skill of this century will not be what you know but rather how quickly and how deeply you can tap into what the people around you know." This great thinker helped us see that the fundamental role of leader is shifting. It is moving away from a model where the leader knows, directs, and tells and toward one where the leader sees, provokes, asks, and unleashes the capability of others.

The world around us is experiencing this shift of managerial tectonics in both subtle and blatant ways. Across the world, we see stark contrasts between governments with Multiplier assumptions and those with Diminisher assumptions at the core of their national logic. We believe that the diminishing cultures we see in organizations, schools, and even families are not inevitable. For these cultures are built on flawed assumptions about how people learn, work, and thrive. As history unfolds, we are witnessing governments and institutions built on the unsteady foundation of diminishing assumptions teeter, suffocate, and collapse. The transition to new models is messy and uncertain, as we see across the world. But in the last analysis, we will find that diminishing cultures are simply unsustainable.

What Is Possible?

Is it plausible that Diminisher assumptions are underlying failing schools? Is it possible for our civic leaders to seed challenges and then turn to the community for answers? Could answers to our most vexing challenges be found through rigorous debate and the extraction of the full intelligence of the community? What would transpire at a school if one principal learned to lead like a Multiplier and found a way to give teachers, parents, and students greater ownership for the success of the school? What if these students and teachers learned these principles together? What if one teacher leader not only led but empowered other teachers to share that leadership? What would happen to families if parents led like Multipliers in their homes?

Is it possible that diminishing leaders can be replaced by those who serve as true Multipliers, inspiring collective intelligence and capability on a mass scale? We need educational leaders who, in times of scarcity, find ways to get more capability and productivity from their current resources. We need professors who are Multipliers to their students and educate a generation of young people who can think critically and enter the workforce prepared to lead as Multipliers themselves. And in times of abundance, we need leaders who can multiply the capability of their colleagues to harness the myriad of opportunities that come from advancements in learning and technology.

It is time for new leadership models—models that allow leaders to harness the collective intelligence of their organizations and channel it into their biggest challenges and opportunities. We need leaders who look around them and see fields of intelligence, ripe for harvesting. We need leaders who can utilize all of the intellect inside our organizations. We need Multipliers, and we need them leading our educational institutions now more than ever.

The Genius Maker

Bono, the rock star and global activist, referring to two prime ministers in England in the 1800s, said, "It has been said that after meeting with the great British Prime Minister William Ewart Gladstone, you left feeling he was the smartest person in the world, but after meeting with his rival Benjamin Disraeli, you left thinking you were the smartest person."[5] We believe this observation captures the essence and the power of a Multiplier.

Which will you be: A genius? Or a genius maker? Are you the sage that is noted for his or her knowledge and smarts, or are you known for releasing the smarts of other? Perhaps you stand with one foot on the building and the other on the wire. Shift your weight. Be the genius maker, and unleash brilliance all around you.

End Notes

1. Benjamin Franklin, *The Autobiography of Benjamin Franklin* (Public Domain Books: 1994). [Kindle edition]

2. The full keynote address can be found at https://www.aamc.org/download/313270/data/aamcpresidentsaddress2012.pdf

3. For a great example of Moses learning to lead like a Multiplier, read the 18th chapter of the book of Exodus in the Old Testament or in the Shemot book of the Torah.

4. "Man on a Wire," DVD 2009, directed by James Marsh, UK, Wall to Wall Productions, 2008.

5. "The 2009 Time 100: The World's Most Influential People," *Time*, May 11, 2009.

Acknowledgments

This book couldn't have happened without the insights and experiences so freely shared with our research team by 108 superintendents, principals, assistant principals, and teachers across the United States, British Columbia, and the United Kingdom. They were our nominators who brought real-life Multipliers into this book. To them we send enormous appreciation for the hours of interview time spent with us on the phone and via email. Thank you for the Multiplier examples you inspired us with, and thank you for the courage to share the Diminisher examples. Without them there would be no book!

This brings us the many Multipliers themselves we studied who inspired both our work and our personal leadership practice. You can check them out in Appendix C. Their professional contributions are compelling and motivating.

Next, there is a group of colleagues who stepped up and took one of the Multiplier Experiments, thus giving us further evidence of the Multiplier Effect. Kudos to Alahrie Aziz-Sims, Van Bowers, Alyssa Gallagher and the Los Altos School District staff, Shekhar Hardikar, Francois Laurent, Cherie Novak, Alice Parenti, Robert Thorn, Jim Vangerud, and Mario Waissbluth for finding time to take on another challenge in an already jam-packed challenging profession.

We acknowledge our critical band of reviewers who read and reread the early versions of this book, helping us write with clarity. Big thanks to Evette Allen, Aaron Anderson, Tracy Brisson, Nick Dennis, Lori Emerick, Susan Foster, Alyssa Gallagher, Steve Hayden, Cate Hiatt, Hazel Jackson, Samantha Jaspal, Neha Kale, Ann Koufman, Cherie Novak, AnnChristin Rothstein, Mark Steed, Jeremy Ward, and Amy Wolfgang. We thank them for their support, their positive feedback, and their courage to tell us when we were off track.

We acknowledge our publisher, Arnis Burvikovs, at Corwin, for seeding the idea of this book and offering an invitation to take the message into schools where it matters most. Next, we recognize the expertise of Desiree Bartlett and Mayan White at Corwin for guiding this book to completion. We thank Shannon Marven at Dupree-Miller for seeing the promise in Multipliers years ago and making this project happen.

To those whose contribution was so essential that we can't imagine having done this without them: Gaila Erickson, at British Columbia Principals and Vice Principals Association, for partnering with us to do research across British Columbia. Lori Emerick, for not only championing Multipliers across Nike around the world, but also helping to take the ideas into the many schools Nike touches. Hilary Benedick, our research assistant, for being "on it" and always brilliant. Patrick Kelly, Multiplier teacher extraordinaire, for his tireless research, insights, and inspiration, without which this book would not have happened. Marcy Lauck, for sharing her expertise on all matters of educational accountability. Michael Horn for your insights on disruptive innovation in education.

Liz would like to personally acknowledge and thank Judy Jung, my assistant, for contributing her talent and energy to this work and for protecting my ability to work on this book. The team of practitioners teaching Multipliers around the world, for their tireless work. Doug Stevenson, for sharing your gift for story-telling and for your Story Theatre method. My sister Evette Allen, for teaching with full heart and soul, persisting in the face of difficulty, and teaching your students to think and work a little harder as they face their own adversity. My children, Megan, Amanda, Christian, and Joshua, for teaching me to lead and to see why having Multipliers in our schools matters. My mother, Lois Allen, who has been a Multiplier to me and countless others. My husband, Larry Wiseman, for believing in the people around him and reminding me that our children "are smart and will figure it out" on the days when I have doubted.

Lois would like to personally acknowledge and thank: My daughter Liz Wiseman, who has always been an educator at heart. Her wisdom, her insights and her deep appreciation of teachers and educational leaders has driven this process. My daughter Evette Allen, who has been a wise counselor to me in this writing process. My educator colleagues who have inspired me by their practice and have taught me by their example, with a particular mention to the administrative "dream team," Diane Dolwig, Don Angelo, and Mike Weir, at Willow Glen Middle School, who really showed me how to do the job.

Elise would like to personally acknowledge and thank: My husband, Chad, also known as "brain number two," who pushed my thinking to the next level and who was always available to offer insights, review materials, and ask the tough questions and without whose help this book couldn't have been possible. My lovely vibrant daughter, Claire, who at 4 inspires me to lead like a Multiplier. You are amazing, especially when asked to access all of your intelligence and stretch your capabilities. I strive to not get in the way of you sharing your gifts with the world. My parents and five brothers, all of whom provided me with a lifetime of space to explore the world. Thanks for inviting me to do hard things.

Together we've enjoyed a rich learning experience studying these leaders and learning from each other as we've dissected, debated, and voiced these concepts. We hope you find a rich learning experience of your own as you and your colleagues explore, debate, and expand on the ideas in this book and unleash genius across your school.

Publisher's Acknowledgments

Corwin would like to thank the following individuals for their editorial insight and guidance:

Molly Broderson, Principal
Achilles Elementary School
Hayes, VA

Kendra Hanzlik, Teacher, Strategist
Prairie Heights Elementary School
Cedar Rapids, IA

Dr. Paul O'Malley
Assistant Superintendent of Business
District Administration Center
Oswego, IL

Appendix A: The Research Process

This appendix contains a detailed account of the methods behind our research. The process is outlined in three phases: (1) research questions and definitions, (2) the research process, and (3) the development of the Multiplier model.

PHASE 1: RESEARCH QUESTIONS AND DEFINITIONS

Research Questions

- In an educational setting, what are the key characteristics (behaviors and mindsets) of leaders who fully utilize the people they lead?
- In an educational setting, what are the key characteristics (behaviors and mindsets) of leaders who underutilize the people they lead?
- What diminishing assumptions are holding back failing schools?
- What is possible if one principal learns to lead like a Multiplier and finds ways to give teachers, parents, and students greater ownership for the success of the school?

Definition of Key Terms

DIMINISHER: A leader of a district, school, team, or classroom around whom people operate in silos, find it hard to get things done, and, despite having smart people to work with, seem to not be able to do what is needed to reach their (or the team's) goals.

MULTIPLIER: A leader of a district, school, team, or classroom around whom people are able to understand and solve hard problems rapidly, achieve their (or the team's) goals, and adapt and increase their capacity over time.

INTELLIGENCE: Intelligence exists in many forms. In 1994, 52 researchers signed a paper where they agreed that intelligence was "the ability to reason, plan, solve problems, think abstractly, comprehend complex ideas, learn quickly and learn from experience. It is not . . . narrow. . . . [I]t is a broader and deeper capability for comprehending our surroundings."[1] Beyond this, we included the ability to adapt to new environments, learn new skills, and accomplish difficult tasks.

PHASE 2: THE RESEARCH PROCESS

Having already gathered extensive data documenting the Multiplier Effect in business and nonprofit organizations globally, we chose to conduct further research in a cross-section of schools. We conducted interviews in schools throughout the United States, the United Kingdom, and in the Canadian province of British Columbia. We included public and private schools in K–12 and in higher education.

Nominators. Instead of trying to identify Diminishers and Multipliers ourselves, we asked successful educational professionals to nominate these leaders for us. We were careful to select successful professions to avoid having data skewed by frustration over personal career challenges.

Researcher-Administered Survey. Nominators rated the Multipliers and Diminishers they had identified on a 5-point scale against 49 leadership practices. These practices were based on standard competency models, popular leadership frameworks, and practices we hypothesized would differentiate Diminishers from Multipliers. We analyzed the results looking for the largest deltas between Multipliers and Diminishers, the top skills and mindsets of Multipliers, and the skills most correlated with the top mindsets of Multipliers and Diminishers.

Structured Interviews. In each interview we asked a standard set of questions that delved into the situation, the actions and mindsets of each of the different types of leaders (Diminishers and Multipliers), and the impact that the leaders' actions had on the individuals we were

---

[1]Linda S. Gottfredson, "Mainstream Science on Intelligence: An Editorial With 52 Signatures, History and Bibliography," *Intelligence* 24, no. 1 (1997): 13–23.

interviewing and/or their colleagues. Interviews were conducted between April and October 2012. Each averaged 60–90 minutes and was conducted in person or by telephone. Our typical format for an interview kept to the following structure:

1. Identification of two leaders: one who stifled intelligence and the other who amplified it

2. Identification of an experience or story working with each leader

3. Context for working with a Diminisher: experience, setting

4. Impact on nominator: percentage of nominator's capability used

5. Impact on group: role played in group process, perception in broader organization

6. Leader's actions: what was done or not done to impact others

7. Result of actions: outcomes, deliverables accomplished

8. Repeat questions 3–7 for the nominated Multiplier

PHASE 3: THE DEVELOPMENT OF THE MULTIPLIER MODEL

We reviewed approximately 250 pages of interview transcripts and collated them for cross-interview analysis. Then we took this theme analysis and calibrated it against the quantitative data we had gathered from the leadership survey. We then compared the data to the data from the original Multipliers research. We then adapted the original leadership model to reflect the distinct leadership characteristics and environment of the K–12 and higher education setting. Additionally, we calculated the average "percentage of nominator's capability used" for Diminishers and Multipliers. These numbers were 40% and 88%, respectively.

After creating the model for educational leaders, we conducted further research by studying how leaders developed Multiplier leadership characteristics. We gave leaders bite-sized Multiplier Experiments to conduct and then tracked their progress. We also selected a number of leadership teams at particular school sites to conduct these experiments collectively. These studies were conducted in North America (United States and Canada), Latin America (Chile, Guatemala, and Puerto Rico), the United Kingdom, and the Middle East (United Arab Emirates).

THE RESEARCH PROCESS

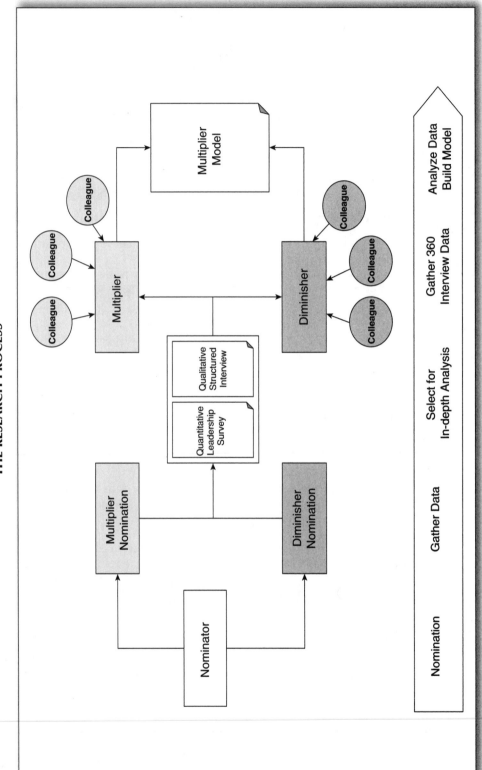

Appendix B: Frequently Asked Questions

Can everyone shift to lead more like a Multiplier, or is there a point of no return?

Anyone who has the ability to look beyond his or her own capability, intelligence, and smarts can begin leading like a Multiplier. However, before the shift can be made, each of us has to recognize the need and make the choice to shift our weight. In our coaching work, we have seen leaders make great shifts from their traditional directive approach toward an approach that accesses the intelligence and capability of those around them.

One leader we studied, Bill Campbell, former CEO of Intuit, started his career as the worst kind of Diminisher. In his early career, he was smart, aggressive, and hard-hitting. He shut people down by saying things like "That's the dumbest question I've ever heard." He began his turnaround when he was confronted by colleagues who told him, "We don't want to leave, but we need to be able to do our jobs." He started listening, respecting the value of others' opinions. Over time, he became a true Multiplier. Today, as a coach of early-stage startup companies, Bill is a Multiplier of Multipliers, asking the hard questions that make others think. His story proves that, with insight and resolve, Diminishers can become Multipliers.

Can you be a Multiplier in a Diminisher culture?

Yes! Many of the Multipliers we studied had worked, or currently work, in diminishing cultures. We find that leading like a Multiplier stems from our personal assumptions about what is possible, rather than the system within which we work. The system certainly plays a role in how Multiplier leadership is received, yet the system can be an easy scapegoat for choosing to take the path of least resistance, or more aptly, the path of the Diminisher. We do recognize that it can be easier to lead like a Multiplier when surrounded by a Multiplier culture. At the same time, part of what inspired us about the Multipliers we studied in education and beyond is that many of them were working in diminishing environments. They recognized that leading like a Multiplier goes beyond the job title or organizational position.

Help, I work for a Diminisher! What do I do?

You can't will your manager to become a Multiplier. For change to be effective and lasting, he or she must have (a) the self-awareness and (b) the interest to lead in a different way. What you can do is minimize the diminishing relationship between you and your leader by changing the dynamics of the situation. Here are two strategies:

1. *Multiply up.* Rather than putting the emphasis on changing your manager's behaviors, work on putting his or her skills to work for you.

   a. *Leverage your boss's genius:* By understanding the strength and skill your manager brings to the situation, you can put that to work and change the dynamic from one of frustration to one of mutual success. If she is a free thinker, could you use her help to brainstorm options for implementing a new school program? If he's got an eye for detail, could you employ his rigor to diagnose the flaws in an important message or proposal to be mailed out districtwide? Ron, a senior executive widely regarded for his own creative genius, was asked to build a new, highly strategic business for Apple. He could have let Steve Jobs, the company's notoriously hands-on CEO, dictate the details of the project, or he could have tried to keep Jobs out of the process as much as possible. Instead, Ron sought out his insights at critical development points. He took the product design to Jobs and openly asked, "How can we make this even better?" Jobs responded not with criticism, but by rattling off numerous ideas for how good features could become great. Ron allowed his team to do their best work without interference, then used the strengths of his boss to take it to the next level. Even if you don't work for a genius like Steve Jobs, you can do the same.

    b. Listen to learn: What happens when you are working with someone who is sucking the energy and intelligence out of you? Often, we find that employees shut down and tune out their leader, especially the criticisms. If you are trapped under a Diminisher, look for opportunities to soften the exchange by actively identifying the points you can incorporate to achieve a better outcome. Too many people go in to meet with their boss "braced for battle" instead of open to see what their boss can teach them.

2. *Multiply yourself:* You don't need to wait to be invited to be smart and to offer your genius. Invite yourself to this party.

    a. Identify, label, and share your own genius: Tell people what you are good at, and offer your capability everywhere it can be of use. Get beyond the walls of your job description, and offer your help in important areas and projects.

    b. Learn from your mistakes: Instead of hiding them, go public and let your school leader know that you've made a mistake (chances are, he or she already knows). Explain where you went wrong, what you learned from it, and how you are going to use this learning with the next class, student, or parent.

    c. Offer to do something hard: Pick something that your school or district leader really needs done, and make yourself really useful.

    d. Play the role of debate maker, even if you aren't the most senior person on the team.

    e. Hold yourself to a standard of completed action: Instead of bringing problems to your leader, bring solutions or concrete recommendations for solutions. (This is also an advantage when you work for a Multiplier!)

Can leaders have both Multiplier and Diminisher traits? Is there something in between?

Leading more like a Multiplier requires strong discipline and a choice to lead with intention. We all can get caught up in our day-to-day responsibilities and temporarily lose sight of how our good intentions might be misinterpreted. So there are times that a strong Multiplier leader may appear to be employing Diminisher approaches. As leaders and educators, it is important that we seek to understand our personal triggers that cause us to take on Diminisher characteristics.

Have you found yourself exiting one meeting energized for having led like a true Multiplier, and yet another admonishing yourself for your diminishing behavior? We find this is quite common, and the reasons are likely one of the following:

We can often be a Multiplier to some and a Diminisher to others. Sometimes we have a tendency to operate differently around different people, unaware. Perhaps we have a history with someone (he's never come through for us) or we simply heard a rumor about someone's ability (Shelly, she's amazing; she'll never let you down). These ideas cause us to take things for granted or expect certain things, and we adjust our behavior accordingly.

Similarly, we might find ourselves in situations that conjure our accidental, or even hard, Diminisher tendencies. This may happen when we find ourselves out of our comfort zone or when we switch roles, like from teacher to coach or teacher to school leader.

The good news is that with these insights in mind, we can begin to lead with intention and minimize our potentially diminishing effect.

In addition, in our continued research across education, industry, and nonprofits, we have found that even extreme Multipliers haven't mastered all five Multiplier disciplines. We also have found that nearly all of us have a tendency to live in the middle of this continuum as an Accidental Diminisher, where despite our best intentions, we limit the capability around us. This can be resolved as each of us continues down the path of thinking in terms of questions and not answers. Begin by challenging yourself with tough questions like these: What are my assumptions about this person's ability to complete a task? Where does my need for control limit others from contributing?

How can I motivate the leaders in my school or district, who are already working overtime, to find the time to be Multipliers?

We often encounter leaders who find themselves operating as Diminishers because they lack the time to be more multiplying. But we also find that when managers operate as Multipliers, they get a huge time rebate. They get to ask the questions and let others figure out the answers. They shift the burden of thinking and accountability for results onto their team more squarely. When these managers do this, they often describe the result as liberating to themselves just as much as to the team.

For example, Samantha Jaspal, head of Haresfoot School and Berkhamsted Pre-Prep at Berkhamsted Schools Group, focused her efforts on giving her team ownership over projects, which was admittedly difficult. What she found was that she freed up more time because people were no longer coming in for bits and pieces. They shifted their thinking from stopping by with "Have you got 5 minutes to discuss this topic?" to "I know we've talked about this, and she's going to ask me what I've thought about it. So I better do all of the thinking before I drop by." Samantha has found herself doing less firefighting and more vision setting.

Leading like a Multiplier is not a matter of adding things to your to-do list; it is a matter of rethinking how you are doing what you already do today. Encourage your leaders by inviting them to experiment with one small practice at a time and see what happens.

What's the difference between deeply leveraging my resources and simply asking them to do more?

This is an important issue, especially as funding and resources become more and more constrained. We know from our research that Multipliers get twice the capability from their staff than do Diminishers. We find they do this by deeply understanding the resources within their organization and aligning genius with the right projects. They are able to get more because they ask for more, not because they tell people they need to give more.

There is a difference between giving people *more* work versus *more challenging* work. Simply doing more of the same work is exhausting; however, being challenged with harder work is exhilarating. Nobody, other than maybe knife jugglers, develops capability by doing more of the same type of work. Widen the gap, appropriately, and your staff will grow to bridge the expanse.

It is important to recognize that your staff comprises many different capability levels, more like a skyline than a horizon. A common mistake is to assume a constant level across the staff and ask for too big a stretch, which causes people to feel like they are just being asked to do more. You might consider the lazy way, and simply ask them to define their own stretches. Most people will define a stretch at just the right level, where they feel pressure but not anxiety.

What do I do if I have an employee who resists Multiplier leadership?

The first question is: Why might this person be resisting? Sometimes, resistance results from a history of diminishing leadership, ancient or not.

Or it might be that people just aren't sure how to respond to a brand-new you. Or finally, it may be a matter of fit. Let's take each of these in turn.

When people become accustomed to diminishing leadership, they may atrophy, forgetting how to contribute at their fullest. Or they may be skeptical of the intent behind your Multiplier motives. To overcome, you might find a need to rebuild trust, especially when this is recent history. Once you are sure trust abounds, which by the way is often a by-product of Multiplier leadership, you may still need to experiment a few times to stoke the fire.

It can be disconcerting to staff members when their leader leaves one day and reemerges with a complete personality overhaul the next. If someone does a 180 with their leadership style, without communicating it clearly, that leader is likely to catch people off guard. Imagine a leader who typically has all of the answers doing an about-face and only asking questions. This may cause you to pull away, rather than lean into the challenge, questions, and debate. Often small steps yield greater results than giant leaps.

Lastly, in the case of improper fit between skills and role, you may need to jointly identify a new position, or pull some weeds—removing low-performing, diminishing staff members. At this point, it may be useful to question your beliefs about this employee. You might ask yourself: How is this person smart? And what can I do to put that genius to work?

What can I do to lead more like a Multiplier today?

There are three distinct points where we recommend you start your journey. The first is to ask your staff, faculty, and students questions that cause them to stop, think, and then respond. To do this, you may consider shifting from more closed-ended questions (like yes/no) to questions that challenge assumptions. As you make this shift, you will begin to see the solution space expand beyond what you and others see as possible—increasing the intrigue and excitement to be involved.

For example, how might the solution space differ between these two questions aimed at improving student learning:

1. How do we reduce class size?

2. How do we get the best teachers in front of the greatest number of students?

In the first case, the prime solution appears to revolve around increasing resources, human and physical. While in the latter, a wider array of possibilities is evident, including the use of technology solutions, altering class size, or addressing teacher capability.

The second point is to construct an environment where debate is embraced, welcoming the input and ideas beyond a critical few. Orchestrate debate on a critical decision. Stand back and witness the sharp and savvy input your colleagues offer. Then lead the school community to drive to a sound decision, rather than making the decision yourself.

Finally, seed the challenge and get out of the way. Take your staff where the action is, allow them to see the opportunities through their own eyes, and then put them in the driver's seat to generate creative solutions.

The Multiplier Experiments and workarounds listed on page 145 in Chapter 7 may prove useful as you select your starting point.

Can you lead like a Multiplier when you are trying to establish yourself in a new role?

When you are new to an administrative role at a school site, everyone will be curious about you and "what you will do to them"! (Remember Amparo Barrera's experience at Hoover Middle School in Chapter 4?) This is the optimal time to establish yourself as a Multiplier—first impressions last a long time.

Everyone will want to drop in to see you in order to check you out. Take this opportunity to turn it around: Check them out! Tell them you want to know what they are good at, what their passion is, what they have outside of their current responsibility and role that they can and *want* to contribute to the school. Then look for opportunities to turn them loose, leveraging their genius to their benefit and the benefit of the school.

What can I do to overcome a low-performing or diminishing individual on my team?

In nearly all of the environments we have studied, people described individuals with personalities that lower the morale and collective intelligence around them. In some cases, you may have the flexibility to reassign or even eliminate this person. But you might also find yourself with few options, if any, wondering what to do. We recognize this is a nontrivial matter in many education settings, where there can be very limited flexibility with regard to staffing.

One place to start might be asking questions such as the following to understand what could be causing their behavior:

- Are they aware that they are perceived negatively by some? If they are aware, what environmental factors, such as coworker dynamics or career history, might be influencing their actions? If they aren't aware, what is the reaction when you have a conversation to help them see the perceptions?
- Has anyone asked them what help they need?
- What opportunity have they had to attend professional development workshops of their choice?
- What have past performance development conversations included? How would they describe what they need to do to improve performance?
- Have they been assigned a performance mentor or coach?
- How have you expressed interest in their career path? What have you done?

Sometimes a series of conversations over time can influence such individuals to shift their behavior, or you to change your own actions in response to their behavior.

Appendix C: The Multipliers

ere you will find an index of the Gold Medal Multipliers high-lighted in this book. While some of these leaders have been featured in numerous chapters, here you will find each listed only for the chapter in which they play the most significant role.

Multiplier	Highlighted Role	Current Role
Chapter 1: The Multiplier Effect		
Dan Baer	Teacher, Montebello Ridge School	Retired; gentleman farmer
Chapter 2: The Talent Finder		
Dana Kauzlarich Miller	Principal, Pioneer Ridge Middle School	Principal, Pioneer Ridge Middle School
Jay Woller	Assistant Principal, Pioneer Ridge Middle School	Assistant Principal, Pioneer Ridge Middle School
Cami Anderson	Superintendent, Newark Public Schools	Superintendent, Newark Public Schools
Dedee Rodriquez	Associate Principal, Willow Glen Middle School	Deceased
Andy Garrido	Interim Principal, Dilworth Elementary School	Retired
Alyssa Gallagher	Assistant Superintendent of Curriculum and Instruction, Los Altos School District	Assistant Superintendent of Curriculum and Instruction, Los Altos School District
Marguerite Hancock	Girls' Camp Director	Associate Director, SPRIE, Stanford University Graduate School of Business

(Continued)

(Continued)

Multiplier	Highlighted Role	Current Role
Chapter 3: The Liberator		
Patrick Kelly	Eighth-Grade Social Studies and History Teacher, La Entrada Middle School	Eighth-Grade Social Studies and History Teacher, La Entrada Middle School
Bill Jensen	Principal, Columbus East High School	Director of Secondary Education, Bartholomew Consolidated School Corporation
Pattie Dullea	Assistant Principal, La Entrada Middle School	Principal, Horral Elementary School
James Garrett	Cofounder and Co-Executive Director, ThinkUnlimited	Cofounder and Co-Executive Director, ThinkUnlimited
Shaylyn Romney Garrett	Cofounder and Co-Executive Director, ThinkUnlimited	Cofounder and Co-Executive Director, ThinkUnlimited
Chapter 4: The Challenger		
Amparo Barrera	Principal, Hoover Middle School	Interim Principal, Alisal School District
CK Prahalad	Professor, University of Michigan	Deceased; beloved teacher and mentor to many
Irene Fisher	Director, Bennion Center	Retired Community Activist; Former Founder and Director, University Neighbor Partners
Linda Aceves	Assistant Superintendent of Instructional Services, Santa Clara County Office of Education	Chief Academic Officer, Santa Clara County Office of Education
Sean Mendy	Director, Center for the New Generation, Boys and Girls Club of the Peninsula	MBA Student, University of Southern California
Bill Green	Principal, Valley View Elementary School, British Columbia	Principal, Valley View Elementary School
Chapter 5: The Community Builder		
Jeff Jones	Superintendent/CEO, School District 8, Kootenay Lake, British Columbia	Superintendent/CEO, School District 8, Kootenay Lake, British Columbia
Lutz Ziob	General Manager, Microsoft Learning, Microsoft Corporation	General Manager, Microsoft Learning, Microsoft Corporation
Allison Liner	Principal, Encinal Elementary School	Chief Learning Officer, Menlo Park City School District

Multiplier	Highlighted Role	Current Role
Brian Pepper	Principal, Heather Park Middle School, British Columbia	Superintendent, School District 57, Prince George, British Columbia
Chapter 6: The Investor		
Jae Choi	Partner, McKinsey & Company	Executive Managing Director, Doosan
Emily Pelino	Principal, KIPP Indy	Executive Director, KIPP Indy
Larry Gelwix	Head Coach, Highland High School, British Columbia	President, California Fresno Mission, Church of Jesus Christ of Latter Day Saints; Speaker
Tom Demeo	Principal, Carihi Secondary School	Assistant Superintendent, School District 71, British Columbia
Kerry Patterson	Cofounder, Interact Performance Systems	Author; Cofounder, Vital Smarts
Chapter 8: Becoming a Multiplier		
Mark Steed	Head, Berkhamsted School	Head, Berkhamsted Schools
Jim Vangerud	Math Teacher and Math Department Chair, Chaska Middle School West	Math Teacher and Math Department Chair, Chaska Middle School West
Cherie Novak	Principal, Robert Fulton Elementary	Principal, Robert Fulton Elementary
Paul Ainsworth	Interim Principal, Belvoir High School	Principal, Belvoir High School
Dr. James Bauck	Superintendent, Eastern Carver County Schools	Superintendent, Eastern Carver County Schools
Sheryl Hough	Principal, Chaska Middle School West	Principal, Chaska Middle School West
Jim Bach	Principal, Chaska Middle School East	Principal, Chaska Middle School East
Jeff Baier	Superintendent, Los Altos School District	Superintendent, Los Altos School District
Dr. Darrell Kirch	CEO, American Association of Medical Colleges	CEO, American Association of Medical Colleges

Index

CORWIN

A SAGE Company

The Corwin logo—a raven striding across an open book—represents the union of courage and learning. Corwin is committed to improving education for all learners by publishing books and other professional development resources for those serving the field of PreK–12 education. By providing practical, hands-on materials, Corwin continues to carry out the promise of its motto: **"Helping Educators Do Their Work Better."**